Prayer in the Shadows

Prayer in the Shadows

Bringing everyday hurts, guilt and fears into prayer

Angela Ashwin

the author of *Heaven in Ordinary*

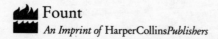 Fount
An Imprint of HarperCollinsPublishers

Fount Paperbacks is an Imprint of
HarperCollins*Religious*
Part of HarperCollins*Publishers*
77–85 Fulham Palace Road,
Hammersmith, London W6 8JB

First published in Great Britain
in 1990 by Fount Paperbacks

3 5 7 9 10 8 6 4

Copyright © 1990 Angela Ashwin

Angela Ashwin asserts the moral right to
be identified as the author of this work

ISBN 0 00 599211 7

Set in Baskerville

Printed in Great Britain by
HarperCollinsManufacturing Glasgow

CONDITIONS OF SALE

All rights reserved. No part of this publication may be
reproduced, stored in a retrieval system, or transmitted,
in any form or by any means, electronic, mechanical,
photocopying, recording or otherwise, without the prior
permission of the publishers.

This book is sold subject to the condition that it shall not,
by way of trade or otherwise, be lent, re-sold, hired out or
otherwise circulated without the publisher's prior consent
in any form of binding or cover other than that in which it
is published and without a similar condition including this
condition being imposed on the subsequent purchaser.

For Vincent

Contents

Preface

I could not have written this book on my own. As well as writing out of my own struggle to pray when things have been hard, I have drawn on the experience and insights of friends, and of others whose words I have read or heard.

I can only thank a few people by name: Sister Rosemary SLG, for her wise comments, Anne Haire and Mary Tomkinson, who have helped me enormously in the sections about illness, and members of the women's group at St Agnes' Church, Burmantofts, Leeds, who used Parts 1 and 2 of this book as a basis for discussion. I particularly value the feedback from Pippa Julings and Liz Schweiger.

I must also thank John White for his poem *Who Shakes a Fist at God*, and many other friends for their quiet and prayerful encouragement during these months of writing.

My children have been marvellously patient, frequently putting up with a harassed and preoccupied mum. I am especially grateful to my husband, Vincent, both for his unflagging support, and for his perceptive criticisms and suggestions about the text.

Unless otherwise stated, biblical quotations are from the *Revised Standard Version*, Second Edition, 1971, and quotations from the Psalms come from *The Alternative Service Book* (SPCK 1980).

Some ideas in this book appeared originally in a series of articles which I wrote for the magazine *Christian* (published by Marshall Pickering), between May 1987 and November 1988.

Angela Ashwin
Newcastle-upon-Tyne
February 1989

Introduction

"*Jesus did not come to explain suffering, nor to take it away; he came to fill it with His presence.*"

Paul Claudel[1]

If Only

Prayer is turning our whole being to God, and staying there.

The trouble is that all sorts of things seem to spoil our attempts to pray, or even put us off praying altogether. You could call them our "if only's":

"If only I wasn't so pressed for time . . ."

"If only so-and-so were not so impossible . . ."

"If only I didn't feel so tired . . ."

"If only I could sort myself out . . . *then* I could pray properly!"

But what we are doing is wishing we could jump over the fence, out of our own garden and into the next, as if our spiritual life would suddenly become marvellous over there! We are missing the fact that God wants us where we are, here and now.

We need to turn our "if only" firmly on its head, and say, "Only this, only now: this is where I will meet God."

It doesn't matter how unsatisfactory or chaotic our lives are; prayer is still possible, because God is not waiting for us to become "worthy" of a spiritual life, or experts in its techniques. He simply asks us to open ourselves up to him, so that he can be given space to love the muddled, selfish person we are. That is what prayer is about: God's love for us, and our response to that love – not our own so-called "spiritual achievements".

If we are honest, there are days when we are so preoccupied or discontented that our prayer is either fragmentary or non-existent. But that doesn't mean that it is hypocritical to read a book like this, or that the kind of prayer I am exploring is beyond ordinary people who have ordinary problems and ordinary bad moods.

Prayer is often bringing to God the things that have been happening over the last few hours or days, during which we may hardly have given him a thought. The last thing we should do is say to ourselves, "I've been letting prayer slip, so there's no point in starting now." There is every reason for praying now: God wants us as we are, not as we think we ought to be.

If we do make an attempt to pray when we are miserable or angry, it can be very hard to concentrate, and familiar patterns of thanks, confession, meditation and so on may seem impossible. That again does not matter. Praying is not an activity which depends on our skill, like sport or cookery. It is coming to God as we are, pain, distraction, ill temper and all.

For everything is raw material for prayer, including the darkest parts of our lives. Even our most unworthy emotions can become prayer's content, prayer's pain, prayer's energy and prayer's joke. Far worse than making a mess of prayer is giving up praying altogether.

This is not to decry the more traditional forms of spirituality. If our lives are going to be rooted in God, we do need some sort of basic pattern of prayer, however often we break it. (The way we work this out in practice will vary according to our circumstances and personalities.) But prayer does not have to end when we finish a "quiet time". It can go on through all of life, including the weary and unhappy blotches on our landscape which you might think were the last things to be part of Christian devotion.

Protest and say "Yes"

It seems a contradiction to say that we should both protest and say "Yes" to God when painful things come our way. But that is the paradox of prayer. Protesting alone could leave us in a vacuum, with nothing other than our misery to hang on to. Just saying "Yes", on the other hand, could lead us into a false piety, where we swept all our true feelings under the carpet and meekly accepted everything unjust and unpleasant as "the will of God".

We need *both* the freedom to explode to God *and* the courage to accept the truth of what is happening to us.

People sometimes see prayer *only* in terms of complaining to God about our problems and asking him to take them away. If he doesn't provide instant relief, they reckon that prayer is not worth bothering with.

But asking for help is only the beginning of prayer, not its end. If God does not immediately remove our difficulties, we have to find a way of working through them; this is where the mysterious business of saying "Yes" to God begins. We do not have to pretend that we feel fine when we do not; nor are we resigning ourselves to the arbitrary whims of a tyrant god. What we are asked to do is turn towards God from the middle of the pain or confusion in which we find ourselves, and say "Yes" to whatever he will do in and through the situation.

It is precisely because this sort of praying is uncomfortable that it is real. And the fact that we are sometimes hurt or anxious brings us close to Christ in his suffering. As Christians, we are called to face our own pain, and the pain of the world, and to hold the whole mess in the powerful love of the crucified and risen Christ, to be healed and redeemed by him.

This is no handbook of easy answers

People are mysterious things.

You can fix a broken leg or deal with a housing problem. But you cannot "solve" a person's grief or sensitivity to pain. You can analyse humans as a collection of bodily cells consisting mostly of water, or as a sociological phenomenon with an average of two-and-a-half children and one-fifth of a nervous breakdown per head. But you cannot sum up a whole person in any set of statistics.

Really to know an individual means entering the mysterious world of love and vulnerability and laughter. It is the things we long for and suffer and create that make us who we are, as unique human beings; these things cannot be quantified.

The closer you are to a person, the more you realise that there is still a vast area inside that you hardly touch. We cannot even know ourselves fully, or begin to plumb the depths of our own subconscious. Hurt, guilt and fear are part of this mysterious side of our human nature, and praying with these things will not provide clear-cut solutions, or techniques guaranteed to remove the pain.

The experience of suffering is part of being alive in this

extraordinary world, where fun, unselfishness and beauty are mixed up with sickening cruelty and devastating disasters. Prayer is not an escape route from the shadows; it is a way of facing them with God.

Reading this book

There are various ways in which this book could be used. The individual sections within each part are deliberately short, so that busy people can pick up and read a section or two at odd moments. It might in any case be helpful to read the book in short doses, perhaps taking one theme each day. At the end of each section there are reflections or quotations, which could lead into prayer. Obviously the reader need not stick rigidly to this suggestion. My own experience with books like this is that on some days I have a particular need, so that I only want to dip into certain parts. At other times I find it stimulating to cover a larger chunk of the book straight off.

We all vary so much in situation and character, that ideas which ring bells with one person will leave another cold. Our moods change, too, so that a suggestion which irritates you on Tuesday may be quite helpful on Thursday. In the end it is God who guides us to pray, in the ways he wants.

* * *

Overheard by the Church Mouse

Christian: *Lord, maybe I ought to do some penances or fasting of some sort; my life's such a mess.*

God: *You've got quite enough difficulty to contend with already; work through that with me, before you think about piling any other uncomfortable things onto yourself.*

Christian: *Lord, I can't do any spiritual exercises until I've got my own problems out of the way.*

God: *But your problems* are *your spiritual exercises. So let's get on with it!*

PART 1

Hurts

Jesus's ordinary, everyday clothes shone, the clothes of work and sweat and travel; His ordinary body was transfigured, the body prone to weariness and pain, and destined to suffer much more. The same is true for us in prayer.

Maria Boulding,
writing about the Transfiguration of Jesus[1]

He Took Bread

The nagging pain we experience when somebody has hurt us can threaten to swamp our feelings and spoil everything we do. Yet a turning-point comes if we can take the pain in both hands and face it, instead of running away from it or letting it overwhelm us.

I was hurt and angry. Some unkind things were being said about me, and I had just heard about a piece of gossip which was the last straw. This was many years ago, and I was on my way to church; I remember going blindly through the porch with tears in my eyes. My prayers before the service were simply an outburst of resentment, and I did not feel in the least bit "religious".

But during that Holy Communion service, some familiar words hit me like a bomb:

"On the night that Jesus was betrayed, he took bread . . ."

He took bread!

Jesus took hold of the bread of his suffering, grasping his own agonising situation, and transforming it into a supremely life-giving and healing act.

"This is my body, broken for you . . ."

At that moment I began to see that there were new possibilities for praying with my own anger and misery.

Up until then I had allowed my hurt feelings to dominate me. But now I didn't just have to be the victim of what had been done to me. There was something I could do myself, by taking hold of my pain, as Jesus had taken hold of the bread.

But could I do it? I felt so battered inside that I was not sure whether I could summon the strength. But then another important lesson struck me. Jesus had already taken hold of my pain, and received it into himself on the cross. I was not alone in this, and God was not expecting me to perform some impossible spiritual feat. He was simply asking if I was willing to try and face my hurt, with him.

"Accepting" is a dangerous word

To say that praying with pain involves facing and accepting the hard things could be misunderstood as spineless submission:

"Let your drunk husband hit you . . ."

"Don't try and stop people taking advantage of you . . ."

"You've just got to put up with oppression!"

But the sort of acceptance that Christ taught us involves standing firm against what is wrong, both in ourselves and others, and taking on board the responsibilities that our situation demands.

I know of a couple who adopted two Bangladeshi babies. At first some members of their own family were highly indignant, and some neighbours even snubbed them in the street. "Acceptance" for this couple did not mean feebly giving in to the pressure of their opponents; it meant being prepared to resist people's opposition and to absorb the sting of racist remarks, as an unavoidable part of being

Mum and Dad to those babies. This was an act of strength, not weakness, and they depended constantly on God in order to keep going.

Facing and accepting our problems may actually increase the pain at first. But the alternative is to run away from ourselves and from God.

There is a parish in the north of England where a small group meet regularly for prayer and Bible study. At one meeting they took the experience "He took bread", which I described above, as a basis for discussion, and shared at a deep level their own experiences of hurt. Then they used some bread as a symbol, to help bring their prayer alive.

Afterwards the leader of the group wrote to me:

It was a particularly potent image for us to see the piece of bread as representing our *own* hurt. I led with the words:

As we share the bread and pass it round, let us see in it our own brokenness. let us take it in both hands, hold it, face it, and remember that Jesus took his broken life into his hands too.

From something as everyday as bread, he saw his mission in a new light – the bread had to be broken before it could be life-giving.

Let us offer our lives, as they are, to be taken up into Christ's suffering love in the world.

* * *

Thank you, Lord, that you understand our emotions and weak-

nesses better than we do. Thank you for showing us how your brokenness has become the way through to new life and healing.

We Need to Explode

Some people are cautious about giving vent to their hurt and bitterness in prayer, because it seems disrespectful to tell God that you can't stand somebody. Yet we must have an outlet for our feelings. Prayer is the supreme opportunity for this, if we have the courage to give God everything, and then stay with him, so that our anger and pain can be redeemed.

It is immensely frustrating not to be allowed to have a good rage about things, or express what we really feel. Logical arguments about why we should not be upset only make matters worse. We need to ventilate our hurts with someone who loves us and won't simply tell us that we ought to pull ourselves together.

If this is so on a human level, it applies even more in our relationship with God. It is when we release our true feelings to him, anger and all, that his grace and love begin to break in.

The problem is that this approach seems irreverent. "You can't say things like that to God!" exclaimed one lady during a discussion about praying with hurts. "You should confess the fact that you feel angry, but that's all!"

I understand what she means, and share her desire to give the best we can to God. But I know that if I did not tell God exactly what I thought, I would be hiding something from him. God does not wait until we are purified of all our rottenness before we can approach him. He wants us as we are, and offers us the freedom to be totally ourselves with him. He knows what is going on inside us anyway, so why try to hold back from him the very things that most need healing?

If we try to avoid life's difficulties, or push them out of prayer, this ultimately increases their hold on us. Bottled-up emotions invariably return as relentlessly as a squeaking Jack-in-the-Box, and they can wreak emotional havoc later. This may come out in some form of depression, or in a smouldering resentment, which can destroy somebody's peace of mind, and flare up in sudden vindictive outbursts against other people.

Another reason why people are afraid to rage and moan at God is that it could seem to be justifying bitterness and resentment. But God will not spoil us or encourage us to be petty and vindictive, as an over-indulgent parent would. We can trust him to make us more the person we were created to be, however painful the purifying process. Pouring out our anger to God reduces its power and clears the air, so that we can then move on to something deeper.

The following sequence may ring bells with some of us. Awkward aged relation: "I'll wash up; no I *insist*! . . . Why on earth do you have so many dishes? When my family were young we only had . . ."

She then sits down to watch early evening TV; she has it on very loud, because she is rather deaf. The noise stops a young child upstairs getting to sleep; the tearful child comes down. Response from the armchair: "*You* ought to be asleep by now." She is unwilling to turn the volume down, so invites the child to watch the programme with her (quite unsuitable!). The child is over-tired and scratchy the next day, and is therefore told off again by elderly relative . . . The bubble bursts in a row, in which Mum is told that she spoils the children.

Most of us in this sort of situation find our prayer life in a considerable state of disarray. The only thing to do is to tell God exactly what we think, and stop trying to pray politely. Churning over a row often makes us think of all sorts of things we wish we had said; but at least we *can* say them to God! Sometimes people find it helpful to write down their grievances, and then literally hold the paper up to Christ, as a prayer for help and forgiveness.

While we are in the full blast of irritating or hurtful circumstances, a well tried way of praying is to use a short phrase, such as, "Lord, this is yours," or "Abba, Father," repeated many times. That may be the only sort of prayer that is real at this stage.

When our indignation has died down a bit, we may be able to pray more reflectively about the situation, and perhaps view things from the awkward person's standpoint – perhaps they feel useless or unwanted. We may also be able to see our troubles in a wider perspective, as part of the pain of the world. But first we must be free enough to be angry.

* * *

The writers of the Psalms also exploded at times:

Contend, O Lord, with those who contend with me:
   fight against those that fight against me.
When I slipped they mocked me:
   and gnashed at me with their teeth.
Let not those that wrongfully are my enemies triumph over me:
   let not those that hate me without cause mock me with
      their eyes.
They stretch their mouths to jeer at me and say,
   'Aha, aha! . . .'
O Lord, do not be silent:
   O God, go not far from me.
Bestir yourself, awake to do me right.

                        (Psalm 35:1, 15, 19, 21–3)

Something Hard to Carry

Persistent domestic hurts can be terribly disruptive to prayer – at least to the ordered and peaceful sort of praying we would like. Even if we do manage to work through a painful clash with God, we may then come straight back to the person we find difficult, so that the goading and irritating start all over again. It seems an endless process of getting hurt and struggling to cope.

We may feel like giving up praying altogether. Forgiveness seems beyond us, we are ashamed of our self-pitying reactions, and feel that we simply cannot be ourselves . . .

A turning point comes when we can see things from a different perspective.

Jim and Margot were going through a rough patch in the middle years of their marriage. Margot was unwell, and had become tense and irritable. She criticised Jim's efforts to help her at home, but complained that she had too much housework to do. She often interpreted innocent remarks as personal criticisms, and accused all the family of being against her. She wanted as much pity as possible from everybody, so she told her friends a lot of half-truths about Jim, letting people think that he didn't care about her.

Jim wondered how much longer he could stand this. His peace with God was shattered, and he felt increasingly guilty about the resentment building up inside him. In desperation he went to see an old friend, and poured out the whole story.

After a pause the older man said, "Tell me exactly what you want to do when she's at her worst."

"I want to shout at her, 'Go to hell, stew in your own juice – I'm going!' " Jim replied. "But I don't really want to do that to her. I long to say it, just to relieve my own feelings, but I couldn't ever pack my bags and go."

"Okay, so that's your immediate reaction. Now carry on, and see if you can put into words what you want for Margot, deep down."

Jim replied slowly, "I suppose I want the best for her; I want her to be herself again, to be happy."

"And that's going to take a lot of healing," continued the older man, "plus a good deal of praying. I think God is asking you to share with him the painful burden of what's going on in Margot. She's all knotted up inside, and every time she hurts you, she is passing on to you a bit of herself which needs healing. You're being given something to carry – like a piece of wood – and it's for her sake.

"When she starts being unkind again, a bit of Margot is coming hurtling across at you, almost like a parcel flying through the air, and landing – womph – in your lap. It hurts, but don't let the pain sour you; see if you can grasp hold of it as a positive act, something you do, as well as something done to you.

"It's as if God is saying, 'Here, will you carry this . . . for Margot?'

"Let's face it, sometimes you'll be so darn mad you will simply want to rebel and shout 'no' at God. And let him have it when that happens! Don't try to hide anything from him.

"But at other times I think you will manage to say 'Yes', though it will take all your strength, and you may wonder how it can possibly be of any use. I reckon that the only prayer being asked of you at the moment is to work through all this with God."

* * *

Eternal life is found not by those who seek the heroic cross, but by those who do not dodge the humdrum one.

Fison[2]

Those Who Bring Out the Worst in Us

Clashes with the people we find difficult throw up a lot of unpleasant elements in our own personality that we would rather not acknowledge. But even self-pity and hostility can be grist to the mill of prayer.

An irritating thing about those who are always finding fault is that there is often an element of truth in what they say. Perhaps we *have* been unwise or forgetful; maybe we *are* inefficient at times. But what hurts and fills us with self-pity is the way people stand in judgement on us, either in streams of nit-picking and interference or in veiled criticisms, through "casual" remarks and comparisons.

When we are blamed or attacked in this way, our first instinct is to leap to our own defence, so that, before we know where we are, we are hurting the other person back. Afterwards we curse ourselves for losing our temper, and ponder, with some dismay, how much insecurity and selfishness there is in us that needs to be healed and forgiven.

Another result is that we may start to become over-sensitive, and exasperate our critical friends by seeing criticism when it was not intended.

Two fires

Two kinds of fire can burn inside us. One is a smouldering fire of resentment, which flares up at any moment and does far more damage to us than to the person who is hurting us. We brood away, justifying ourselves, and indulging in numerous day-dreams in which we have the satisfaction of putting other people firmly in their place.

The other kind of fire is difficult to kindle by ourselves, but God can kindle it in us when we pray. It is a fire which consumes the rubbish of self-centredness, and clears enough space for us to be able to admit our mistakes. There is a sense of freedom, almost lightness of spirit, when we can see beyond our blistering indignation to the things that we need to watch in ourselves.

God is not one of the fault-finders; he harbours no mean or vindictive thoughts against us. So there is nothing to fear in facing our faults with him.

We still wince when the next tirade of blame comes: "Here we go again," we think to ourselves, "now what have I done?" We may have to pray through this pain many times if somebody has a chip on the shoulder concerning us. But it is not necessarily a bad thing when we see how hurts from others bring out the worst in us. Dark sides of our nature are surfacing which might never otherwise have been opened up to God, for him to redeem and transform.

* * *

Lord, I thank you that you understand me totally.
Burn away the resentment in me.

You know how unkind and unjust the things are which have been said. Help me to see clearly which aspects of my own behaviour I should look at as well.
Am I prepared to expose my weaknesses to you, honestly?
Lord, use the pain to purge away a bit more of my pride.

"To be redeemed from fire, by fire."

T. S. Eliot[3]

The Pain of Criticism

'Reputation' is a particularly heavy piece of luggage to carry round, and it is good to be free of it. Ideally we should be able to travel light with both praise and blame, but that is easier said than done.

Most of us feel uneasy when people disapprove of us or of our opinions. We want to be liked and accepted, and tend to assume that we have a right to be completely understood, whereas this is in fact a luxury which we will only occasionally enjoy.

We may be so obsessed with preserving an untarnished reputation, that we become like a circus-artist, frantically dashing round keeping numerous plates spinning on rods. But we must stop trying to please everybody. What people think of us doesn't matter a fig.

It is revealing to imagine a scenario which is the opposite of being unpopular: suppose everybody worshipped the ground we walked on! Would we really be happy? I doubt it.

Praying with criticism is an opportunity to ask God to prune us of some of our pride. Many of us still go pink at the gills when people disagree with us aggressively, especially in public. And we only have to receive a cutting remark based on ignorance, or a letter which makes unjust assumptions about us, for a wave of indignation to sweep through us once more. It helps if we can see the funny side of our desire to present an undented image to the world. As a wise friend once said to me: "It doesn't matter whether they think you're a hag or a honey."

The fact that we dislike being misunderstood should not, however, make us feel guilty. It is natural to feel this way. The question is really about our priorities. Does our concern for approval take up too much of our attention, and overrule other, more important things? When we realise how infinitely we are loved by God, our craving to be loved and accepted by other people becomes less vital. This is one of the many reasons why prayer helps.

Horatio

I have a name for my fear of disapproval: Horatio. When I start worrying about what people think of me, I can say to myself, 'Now then, Horatio! I know you!'

Horatio is a comic character, a pompous ass strutting around the stage. He fusses and flaps when he thinks he might be offending anybody, and will drop hints about an easy way out if any conflict appears on the horizon.

Trying to bully old Horatio into submission doesn't work; he always pops up again. It is better to laugh at him with God (in other words, laugh at myself), putting him next to the infinite stature of Christ. Then the huffing and puffing Horatio is cut down to size.

Through prayer God makes our Horatios harmless, loving them out of business, and giving us courage to be ourselves.

* * *

God looks at each of us with the eyes of love. Other people look at us with their own particular squint, and often have only a partial understanding of who we are.

   God knows us,

      God accepts us, as we are,

         God forgives us,

           God loves us.

That is what matters.

"Spirituality is not concerned with our defences, but with their removal."

Alan Ecclestone[4]

Irritation – a Yes Which Hurts

Few emotions threaten to sabotage our praying as efficiently as irritation. Somehow we have to find a way of bringing our irritated feelings into prayer, so that they can become something constructive.

The following piece of fiction illustrates the problem.

David got up early, and went into the sitting-room to have a time of quiet with God before going to work. The room stank; a stray cat must have come in through the cat-flap during the night. David remembered the previous evening's conversation: his wife had wanted to leave the flap open because the cat was out, and it was frosty. He had warned her that there was a stray tom-cat in the garden, but to no avail.

He shouted upstairs, "I knew this would happen; there's a foul smell of cat down here!"

A voice emerged from the bathroom, "Sorry" (the tone of voice showing that she obviously didn't mean it.) "Anyway you should have shut the inside kitchen door." Slam!

Increasing irritation came over David as he tried to pray. He attempted to concentrate on a passage from Jeremiah, but nausea crept over him because of the smell. So he decided to give up and go for a walk, praying as he went. But still the irritation bugged him . . .

Sometimes our irritation is quite unjustified; we are niggled because someone sniffs, or moves rather slowly, or dotes on budgies. At other times we are irritated over things which are genuinely wrong, when people do not pull their weight, or when they leave an untidy mess for others to clear up.

However justified or not our feelings may be, the surge

of irritation still has to be handled. How do we pray with it? Bible readings seem irrelevant and concentration is almost impossible.

It helps to ask ourselves why we are so rattled. What is it that matters so much to us, to have disrupted our inner peace?

This is a revealing exercise. All kinds of things may have been spoiled or threatened by the other person. It could be a selfish concern, such as our routine or our reputation as a home-maker; or it might be the well-being of a friend, or the aims of a movement we support.

Suppose you are irritated because your friend is ill and her family have not bothered to visit her, even though they live nearby; or you wrote to the newspaper about a local injustice and they only printed half your letter, so that you appeared to be saying the opposite of what you meant.

In such situatons, that irritation can be made into a prayer, a "Yes" to those things which matter: our friend's welfare, the neighbourhood issue. The pain of irritation is the cost of caring.

Other causes which have burned so fiercely in our breast will cease to be so important to us when we expose them to the light of God. Is it really so vital who gets coffee first in the office, or how short or long our children's hair is? Does it matter that our public esteem is affected? A "Yes" to God in these circumstances is not easy. It is a "Yes" to the dent in our pride and comfort, a "Yes" to the irritation itself.

We don't like it; but facing irritation this way can be a kind of purifying – by God's grace – so that we become a fraction more the loving, self-forgetful person we were meant to be.

This sort of scene may be familiar . . . I am extremely tired, and I have a rare chance for a lie-in; but somebody telephones at eight a.m. and wakes me up.

How do I pray with my irritation?

I need to ask myself the question: What is the issue that matters so much to me? My need of sleep? Perhaps. But what about X who woke me up? Can I say "Yes" to her, accepting her as she is, or do I expect her to be perfect? God accepts me constantly, as I am, with all my irritating and selfish habits. Am I like the servant in the parable in Matthew 18:23–35, refusing to forgive somebody this one tiny thing, when I myself am forgiven so much? Do I only accept people on certain conditions? Am *I* so perfect?

I *shall* probably mention this incident to her, and ask her to ring a bit later on Saturdays. But, for the present, I am asked to take on board the chafing irritation inside me; it is something of her that has rubbed off onto me. As well as protesting I must also say "Yes," in this costly business of loving.

To return to the cat-beleaguered husband. What matters most?

A pleasant, sweet smelling home . . .?

The desire to establish that he was right and his wife wrong . . .?

Accepting that his wife is human and sometimes makes mistakes of judgement . . .?

Accepting *her* . . .?

* * *

Prayer is the battlefield in which we conquer by letting God conquer.
S. Kierkegaard (1813–1855)

Come, O Christ my Light, and illumine my darkness.
Come, my Life, and revive me from death.
Come, my Physician, and heal my wounds.
Come, Flame of divine love, and burn up the thorns of
    my sins,
Kindling my heart with the flame of thy love . . .
For Thou alone art my King and my Lord.
St Dimitri of Rostrov (17th century)[5]

Outrage

How do you pray when you get home from a holiday to find the place burgled and ransacked? Most of us would say, "I don't!" But after we have raged at everyone and everything, and sorted out some of the chaos, we may calm down sufficiently to ponder in prayer what our possessions mean to us.

It feels as if you have been violated yourself when you find that burglars have been through all your belongings, especially if they damaged or stole articles which were precious to you for personal reasons. And it can take ages to clear up the mess.

"Prayer?" you utter in amazement. "You must be joking!"

I'm not. Scream at God. Let it out. If you hang on to

your anger and nurse it the devil has won, because you are letting what happened poison you. Pour out your fury to God for as long as you need to. This is supremely a time when accepting the situation means putting rebellious feelings into words. Later on, other ways of praying may be possible, because being burgled throws into sharp relief what really matters to us.

Losing an object given to me by somebody I care about is part of the pain of loving; can I make my pain a "Yes" to that love? Losing my video is an irritation which hits those of us who have the luxury of choosing whether or not to possess such marvellous gadgets. Can I make my loss into a "Yes" to the huge privilege and responsibility of being a first-class passenger on this planet?

To ponder

● Before I was born, my clothes, meals, name and living-place were all decided for me, and I entered this world with empty hands and a good deal of indignity.

● When I die people will go through all my belongings anyway, possibly with respect, possibly not.

● How much do I depend on my possessions and my dignity? Am I willing to ask God to make me more detached, and therefore more free?

● My possessions are not me; people can violate my house, but they cannot violate me unless I let them.

● To imagine that I have absolute power over "my" things or my fortune is an illusion, as I discover only too well when my wallet is stolen or illness wrecks my plans. The rich landowner in Jesus's parable realised too late how futile it had been to put all his security into barns full of hoarded goods. He had said to himself, "Soul, you have ample goods laid up for many years; take your ease, eat, drink, be merry!" But God said to him, "You fool! This night your soul is required of you; and the things that you have prepared, whose will they be?" (Luke 12:16–20).

● The more I let go, the less I have to lose. Nobody can take from me the things that really matter.

* * *

Lord Jesus,
I give you my hands to do your work.
I give you my feet to go your way.
I give you my mouth to speak your words.
I give you my mind that you may think in me.
I give you my goods that you may share through me.
And I give you my spirit that you may pray in me,
so that it is you, Lord,
who live and move and have your being in me. Amen.
(Based on a prayer in a sixteenth-century Book of Hours)

Deep Wounds

What do you do with the surge of emotion against someone who deliberately works against you out of jealousy and spite, or who is vindictive to your face or grossly dishonest behind your back? Trying to pray at such times is a long, hard night of the spirit. As well as working through our reactions, both worthy and unworthy, we need to face a crucial question: do we want hatred to dominate the way we live from now on?

A deep hurt can inflict an open sore, which we carry round all the time and hardly ever get out of our mind. It is a relief when we find we have forgotten about the trouble even for a few minutes. We do not feel at all inclined to love the person who has wounded us, and perhaps the only prayer we can honestly muster is, "O God, I hate him/her. Forgive me." But it is when we have unlocked our feeling to God that we can ask him for help. And that help often comes in the form of a question: "Do you want to hate that person above all else?"

"Wanting-not-to-hate" may be the nearest we can get to loving at this stage. It may not seem much, but it is vital. That tiny spark of desire against the power of hatred is the work of the Holy Spirit in us, however muffled and disguised it may be.

If we offer the whole mixed bag of our desires and emotions to God, he helps us to sift out the more selfish side of our nature, which simply wants revenge, from our better self. A candle is a useful aid to prayer when somebody's unkindness is almost too much. The flame can symbolise our deeper desire that our anger will be purged by God's fire of love, in spite of our considerable surface resentment.

But we are unlikely to mop up our bitterness in one go by praying like this. It is unnerving how waves of hatred keep coming over us, especially if the hurtful person goes on to inflict some fresh wounds. Our feelings have to be offered to God again and again, often with tears and a sense of despair, wondering if we will ever get on top of our unhappiness.

But Christ is with us in this darkness. Absolutely nothing can separate us from his love. When he rose from the dead and appeared to the disciples, he did not have a totally other-worldly body, untouched by the pain of human life. Jesus was still wounded, and made a point of showing those wounds to the disciples (Luke 24:19; John 20:27).

He still bears those marks today, with us and for us, and when we pray with our hurts we can place our wounds in his. This is not easy, and it is right to be suspicious of easy platitudes about "radiant sufferers" or "pain-made-easy". What *does* matter is that we keep on bringing everything to him, even through the most miserable times.

You may like to join me in imagining a scene where a few hundred people of many nationalities, young and old, are sitting in a large, round church singing a simple chorus: "Jesu Christe, Miserere; Jesus Christ, have mercy."

It is dark outside, but as you come through the door you are struck by the warmth and mellow light coming from candles held by everyone. There are also candles placed round a large, central picture (an icon) of Christ on the cross.

The singing stops, and a young man from Nicaragua stands and leads a prayer for his country, describing the suffering of his family, many of whom have been killed. The prayer is translated into several languages. There is more singing. Then a woman from Northern Ireland quietly and movingly holds before God the agonies of her community. This, too, is translated, and another song follows.

Then there is a period of silence, when everyone offers to Christ their own individual pain, as well as that of all the world.

There is a profound sense that Jesus is there, sharing the torment and frustration, and soaking up the cruelty and bitterness of the human race. But there is also the conviction, deeper than words, that Jesus's love is a power stronger than all evil, and that his resurrection gives us ultimate hope.

For some people, a way of praying with pain is to go through and beyond it into silence.

If someone has wronged you, picture the hurt still thrashing around inside you like a spiked wheel. From each spike fly out sparks of rage and anger, words of self-pity, words of revenge, words of self-justification. Imagine the spiked wheel gradually slowing down and stopping. Let your pain become focused into a clear, single stab of pain. Face it; sit still with it.

Then hold the pain up to Christ on the cross, in an offering without words. By doing this you give him the whole package, your wounds and your own failings. It is his pain as well as yours.

There is a silence in the heart of suffering. Stay there in the stillness, vulnerable and exposed, so that the pain becomes the point where God touches you most deeply.

* * *

I will face this,
I will accept its full impact,
silently
turning my gaze
onto the crucified Christ,
who is in the darkness with me.
I am enfolded and held in the love of God
who is both Love-in-death and Love-Risen.

A Vital Link in Forgiveness

There is a strange link between us and the person hurting us, which puts us in a unique position to pray for them. Forgiving also brings us closer to God himself.

Iulia de Beausobre, a Russian Christian imprisoned in the 1930s after the Bolshevik revolution, said that, when she was being tortured, she had a curious sense of being closer to her torturer than anyone else in the world. Receiving such a stream of cruelty from him, she was in direct contact with the evil inside him, and could therefore pray for him at a very deep level. She also knew that the pain was shared by Christ, and felt a strong sense of "participation" with him in the "suffering and the redeeming of the deed".[6]

Such heroism is beyond most of us. Yet Iulia's story is a parable illustrating a mysterious fact. We have a unique opportunity to pray for the healing of a person who wrongs us, because our hurt has opened up a direct channel of contact between us. Our pain can be the point where God's love meets that person, through prayer. This is God's doing, not ours.

What is forgiveness?

Forgiveness means poverty on our part and activity on God's. We have to let the pain carve out a channel in us, rather than cause a blockage. Dirt and rubbish accumulate in blocked pipes, so that a whole system is poisoned. But a hollowed-out channel allows God's energy of healing and reconciliation to be released.

Hurts can fill us with bitterness, or else clutter us up with a self-satisfied magnanimity: yes, we will, from our pedestal, condescend to pardon them. Forgiveness, we suppose, is a thing that we will summon from our own resources, and graciously bestow on the guilty party – as long as they are duly penitent, of course.

But this is comic self-deception, and life will not always give us a fair deal. True forgiveness means allowing the other person to be free, and letting go of our desire to extract the apology which we see as our right. It means being sufficiently empty and "poor in spirit" to be a channel of God's gift of mercy, even when the wrong against us has not been redressed.

This prayer was found in 1945 on a scrap of paper beside the dead body of a Jewish child in the Nazi concentration camp at Ravensbruck, where 92,000 women and children died.

O Lord,
remember not only the men and women of goodwill,
but also those of ill will.
But do not only remember the suffering they have
   inflicted upon us,
remember the fruits we bought thanks to this suffering,
our comradeship, our loyalty, our humility,
the courage, the generosity,
the greatness of heart which has grown out of all this.
And when they come to judgement
let all the fruits that we have borne
be their forgiveness. AMEN. AMEN. AMEN.[7]

* * *

In human life there is nothing more welcoming and transparent to the presence of God than an attitude of forgiveness. It opens wide the gates for God. In forgiveness God and human life touch, harmonise, melt together. There the human being is in God's likeness, and a creator with God. (Letter from Taizé)[8]

St Stephen was supremely in a position to pray for the Jews of Jerusalem, because he was on the receiving end of their venom.

As they were stoning him, he prayed, "Lord Jesus,

receive my spirit." And he knelt down and cried with a loud voice, "Lord, do not hold this sin against them" (Acts 7:59–60).

Forgiving on Behalf of Others

Some people say that you cannot forgive those who hurt your friends, because that is your friends' job, not yours.

But this is an over-simplification. We belong to one another, and when somebody I love is hurt, I am hurt too. If I do not forgive, I will always be nursing bitterness on behalf of the person I love. That cannot be right.

It is not a matter of doing our friends' forgiving for them, in a crude exchange. We are called to pray for forgiveness with them and because of them; doing this can only help to release the healing power of God in them as well.

"I can forgive those who hurt me, but not those who hurt my children." So say many of us. It is arguably the greatest torture of all to witness cruelty inflicted on our family. Even comparatively minor hurts to our children can make us very angry.

Some time ago I collected my seven-year-old son, Andrew, from school, and took him to the newsagent's to buy a bar of chocolate for his father's birthday. I then told him I would stand outside while he made the purchase, because I had to look out for my daughter, who was coming home from a different school.

As I was coming out of the shop door, turning round to reassure Andrew that I would not be far away, a lady in a hurry pushed past me with a glare. Fair enough! I was in the way.

I waited and waited outside; the impatient lady came out again, followed by some teenagers. Still no Andrew.

Eventually he emerged in tears: "Mummy, the lady pushed in front of me, and then some girls did too. And I still haven't got Daddy's present . . ."

I felt a wave of dislike against this woman; how dare she take advantage of MY SON?! I was surprised by the strength of emotion which swept through me.

Going through all this later in prayer, two things came clear.

First, by hurting Andrew, that lady had hurt me. To distinguish between hurting me and hurting someone I love would be a nonsense. When somebody else is wounded, I am wounded too. Whether I like it or not, I am involved with all those who are abused and oppressed, in the process of letting God's forgiveness into the matter. I cannot wash my hands of the situation, or say, "It's not for me to pray for the forgiveness of football hooligans or that military régime . . ." We are all caught up in the hurt and healing of the world.

Secondly, I knew I must do something with this rush of indignation. I could at least offer to God my churned-up state over such a small incident; for the victims of the huge injustices of the world; for peasants struggling under corrupt rulers; for families of hostages; or for refugees who see soldiers destroying food lorries that could save their children.

The harder questions

But what if your daughter has been raped by a man with Aids? What if your child was a victim of the horrific "Moors murders" in the 1960s, or if a drug-pusher has persuaded your teenager to take heroin? Can we presume to talk about forgiveness to people facing that sort of hell?

It would be cruel and insulting to say to such parents, "You really ought to forgive, you know." Such talk makes forgiveness sound like an achievement, produced out of our own resources like a bottle of wine out of the cellar.

Forgiveness is *not* pretending that things don't hurt after all, in a layer of sentimental religious blancmange spread over evil deeds. Forgiveness is God's gift; we are its channels, not its creators.

Somebody once asked me, "What would you say, as a Christian, to the parents of murdered children?"

I think I would want to say, in fear and trembling, "I cannot imagine the depths of anguish you have gone through. But when things happen to hurt *my* children, they link me with you in a tiny way, so that I can offer my hurt to God for you.

"Over what they did to your children – what can I say, except that I hate with you and grieve with you and ask the question 'Why?' with you?

"But I also reach out to God for healing of the terrible pain in you. When I try to forgive the people who hurt my children, I'm feeling what I'm feeling *for you* as well as for myself and my own family.

"I'm not saying that you ought to forgive; no one has the right to impose that on you from the outside. I stand empty-handed with you, praying for the power of God's love, instead of the hate which can destroy us both. All I have to offer you in the end is my weakness, and the fact that I care."

The paradox

Can we hold together anger and forgiveness, at the same time?

I think we have to.

If we try to forgive a person who has harmed us or other people, it does not mean that we stop being angry about the wrong that was done. There are, of course, different kinds of anger. Smouldering revenge needs to be healed and purged. But if goodness and truth and love have been violated, we should find ourselves sharing in what has been called God's "wrath" or "righteous indignation" (though a better term would perhaps be something like "burning sorrow").

Jesus rebuked the Pharisees and scribes, and stormed through the Temple in anger at what the Jewish establishment had become. Yet he prayed for their forgiveness when that same establishment engineered his death.

Forgiveness is not a feeling, it's a fact.

Mary, Jesus's mother, must have plumbed the depths of torment and grief when she stood watching her son's cruel death. Looking down from the cross, Jesus saw that she needed a strong and comforting arm round her, and, probably, a shoulder to cry on. So he asked John, his disciple, to look after her: "Woman, behold your son." "John, behold your mother." (John 19:25–26)

I cannot believe that Mary, in her anguish, was vowing revenge against us, the human race, who crucified him. Grief can co-exist with a willingness to forgive. It is right to allow ourselves to feel the hurt fully, and even to feel the *desire* to hit back. But the crucial question is whether we then let these emotions become destructive forces in our behaviour. God's grace can make it possible for us to find resources of generosity in ourselves, even as we experience the terrible battering waves of pain and grief.

I would guess that the depth of forgiveness in Mary was a unique example of this.

* * *

As they crucified him, Jesus said, "Father, forgive them, for they know not what they do" (Luke 23:34).

Healing and Childhood

Forgiving people who hurt us is easier when we picture them as little children.

The late Bishop Leonard Wilson was tortured by the Japanese in Singapore during the Second World War. On some days he was hung upside-down in the blazing sun; he was also whipped while lying face-upwards on a table. He spoke afterwards on the radio about his experience.

. . . I looked at their faces as they stood round and took it in turns to flog me, and their faces were hard and cruel, and some were evidently enjoying their cruelty. But by the grace of God I saw those men, not as they were, but as they had been. Once they were little children playing with their brothers and sisters, in those far-off days before they had been conditioned by their false nationalistic ideals; and it is hard to hate little children . . .

I knew it was only common sense to say "Forgive"..[9]

I know someone who finds it helpful when people are selfish, rude or unkind, to imagine what they looked like as babies or toddlers. Somehow that takes the sting out of the situation and reduces everyone to an equal level.

I tried that once. But the picture which came to mind was of a nasty, pampered, sweet-stuffing little horror, screaming for its own way and getting it. "Humph!" I thought, so much for that exercise.

But then it struck me that the child in my mind was behaving like that largely because the parents had spoiled him/her. And I tried going back further and looking at the new-born baby in the bath! This helped a lot, and I realised how infinitely loved by God that person has always been, and still is.

* * *

They even brought babies for him to touch; but when the disciples saw them they scolded them for it. But Jesus called for the children and said, "Let the little ones come to me; do not try to stop them;

for the kingdom of God belongs to such as these" (Luke 18:15–16 NEB).

Old Hurts

Even if we have done our best to forgive, a wrong done to us will not necessarily stop hurting. We may have to pray through old hurts again and again over a long period of time.

People often feel guilty when harsh memories keep returning, as if there is something wrong with their efforts to forgive. But there is no need to feel that. Forgiving does not automatically mean forgetting. If it did, forgiveness would be easy and shallow, instead of the costly thing it really is.

Most of us carry round a portmanteau of grievances and sore memories which are remarkably difficult to shed. Something only has to remind us, and we start reliving the whole business all over again.

If a hurt from the past comes to mind, it is generally best to receive the pain head-on and let it flow through us. Pushing it away will only make the wound fester in our subconscious. Some people have benefitted greatly from imagining Jesus standing beside or behind them when they remember the painful scenes. Others do not find imaginative prayer helpful, and have to make do with just being there, "feeling silly and lumpish" as a friend of mine once put it, and letting that be prayer.

You sometimes read about sudden transformations in

people's lives when they have opened up the past to Christ and asked for his healing to pour into them. That is tremendous, and we should praise God for it. Yet this does not happen for everybody, and it is a tragic distortion of Christian healing if people are made to feel guilty because they are still hurt by past wrongs, after praying for inner healing. God works in each of us differently, and it may be that he wants us to work more slowly through the pain, by feeling it *with him*.

If we have genuinely *wanted* to forgive, that basic desire still stands, no matter how many painful memories continue to shake us.

Many hurts damage people for a long time after the actual deed. None of us can deal with past, present and future in one go. As the repercussions hit us we have to face them one at a time. We are all in the middle of the process between forgiveness's birth and its ultimate fulfilment, in God's mysterious time beyond time. As long as we keep offering our memories to God, guilt is the last thing we should feel when old wounds continue to take their toll.

* * *

Lord, this is what happened . . .
I give it all to you, every detail, every hurt, the big things
and the petty things;
Let the pain I feel be for healing, and not a spring of bitterness.
Make my wound Christ-centred and for people,
rather than self-centred and against them.

Jesus said, "Peace is my parting gift to you, my own

peace, such as the world cannot give. Set your troubled hearts at rest" (John 14:27–28).

Remember or Forget?

Forgetting is like sleep. You can never force it to happen. And the more you try to do it, the less likely you are to succeed.

To forget about past hurts is a gift, which is more likely to come if you have exposed the painful memories to God first.

A young man who had been beaten up once said that it was no use trying to escape from the memory of the attack. Instead he had to face it, and, by doing so, was able to help other people who had been mugged to come to terms with their emotional wounds and loss of confidence.

On the other hand, a Jew who suffered terribly in a Nazi concentration camp says that he only finds peace when he can forget what was done to him.

Which of them is right? Should we remember, or should we forget? Should prayer take us into old hurts or away from them?

I think the answer is, *both*. Remembering and forgetting are both things that happen to us, rather than things we should try to force on ourselves.

When hurtful events from the past invade our prayers, it can do more harm than good to try and repress them. We may need to "run through the spool" of those experiences many times before the wounds begin to heal.

But after going through the story with God yet again, it is generally best to place the whole hurtful business in his hands, so that we are not totally dominated by it. It helps to have something specific to which we can turn our attention, like a Bible passage or meditation. Then the forgetting which heals is more likely to come.

In my own experience, I was only able to start forgetting some very deep hurts from the past when I poured out all the details to a wise and trusted priest, in the context of the sacrament of confession. (It took about half an hour, so I sat down instead of kneeling!)

That night I woke in the early hours, with the words "It is redeemed" burning in my mind. (I don't normally go in for voices and visions and suchlike, but this was very clear.) My eyes fell onto a crucifix on the wall of my bedroom, and I knew that Jesus had indeed dealt with the source of much past unhappiness and resulting depression. It was as if forgiveness and healing were pouring down from the cross into all those past events, in some way beyond my comprehension.

The old hurtful memories are still sparked off from time to time. But now it is not just a destructive pain; it is a redeemed pain, which I believe heals not only me, but also the people who hurt me.

It was prayer and sacrament together which enabled me to receive this gift of Christ's healing power in such a deep way. Other people will experience differently the same reality – that Christ is ultimately stronger than all evil.

* * *

Lord, delve deeply into my being,
and make me Your dwelling-place,
where all darkness is penetrated by Your light,
all troubles calmed by Your peace,
all evil redeemed by Your love,
and all pain transformed in Your suffering.
          (Based on a prayer by Jim Cotter)[10]

When Someone has not Forgiven You

Much is said, rightly, about the need to forgive others and let go
of old resentments. But what if a person holds something against
you, in such a way that you feel powerless to do anything about
it?

God does not usually rally in spectacular fashion to "vindicate
our cause" or "crush our foes beneath our feet". He seems to do
the opposite, enabling us to find peace by leaving the other person
free to forgive us or not, as they will. This is not weakness; it
is strength, beyond our capacity alone, but possible with God
when we stay close to him.

Many of us face the unpleasant experience of not being
forgiven at some point in our lives. People nurse a grudge
against us over some mistake we have made or wrong we
have done them, and nothing we do by way of apology
seems to soften their resentment.

In numerous families, relatives have flatly refused to talk
to each other for years, and only been reconciled when one

of them was on a death bed, if then. A surprising number of people live in a state of permanent bitterness against somebody.

Praying with the knowledge that we have not been forgiven is hard, because we easily slip into self-pity and a string of arguments about how unreasonable people are. We do need to get these things off our chest, perhaps several times. But then we have to shake ourselves free of them, and widen our horizons.

Even Jesus was sometimes unforgiven. His fellow townsfolk in Nazareth couldn't bear it when he stood up in their synagogue and proclaimed that he was fulfilling the hopes of the Old Testament; they were so furious that they tried to kill him (Luke 4:16–30). Many of the scribes and Pharisees found it impossible to forgive Jesus for apparently undermining their sacred Law.

I would guess that the families of some of the disciples also resented the demands that Jesus made. What did Peter's wife think about Jesus taking her husband away from his home and work? And I wonder if Judas's wife and parents ever forgave Jesus for what happened to him (Matthew 27:3–5)?

Obviously the things people held against Jesus were not blunders or sinful acts on his part, whereas we are mistake-makers and sinners. But it does help to remember that we are not alone in the painful experience of not being forgiven.

Sometimes we may feel as if the person with a grudge against us has some power over us. *But that power is only there if we consent.* God is our only judge. We are not ultimately answerable to any human being, but to him. He understands, accepts and forgives us, and that is what matters. His mercy is like a fire which consumes and disintegrates the bitter wood of other people's resentment, which may have lodged itself inside us.

This is an imaginary situation. Two sisters in their fifties live together, and find that they are increasingly getting on each other's nerves. The atmosphere at home is so bad that Moira, the younger one, decides that she must have some time away. So she goes to stay with a friend.

Two weeks later, while Moira is still away, her sister, Jocelyn, commits suicide. Moira is devastated, and feels she will never rid herself of her burden of guilt over this. Because Jocelyn is dead, it seems that all possibilities for reconciliation are finally closed.

Moira has to embark on the long, painful process of saying "Yes" to this terrible pain. Her anguish is not meant to be a remorse which will destroy her; God has dealt with her sins, and she is forgiven. But she has to bear the pain *for Jocelyn*. It is as if Jocelyn handed over to Moira a great burden of unhappiness, which she herself could not carry any longer in this life. If there was an element of spite in Jocelyn's action – to make Moira feel guilty – the sting will be lessened by Moira's accepting the pain for Jocelyn's sake. Moira's "Yes" is a way of letting Jocelyn go, letting her be free to move on into something new.

Moira is worried because the possibility of reconciliation seems to have been destroyed for ever. But God's time is not the same as ours. A thousand years are "as one day" with him (2 Peter 3:8). His forgiveness is beyond the narrow limits of our planet's space and time, and Moira need have no fear that a grudge would be held against her into eternity.

* * *

Set your troubled hearts at rest, and banish your fears . . .
Be assured, I am with you always, to the end of time (John 14.27; Matthew 28:20, NEB).

"God said to me, 'I am mercy within mercy within mercy'."[11]

Part of Something Bigger

Our hurt is part of the pain of the world. We are not little isolated units of human existence, each grinding along its lonely track. When one person is damaged, we are all affected, because of our shared humanity.

Praying with our own pain can be a way of acknowledging this essential link between us and others who are suffering in a million different ways. When we bring our troubles to God for the sake of the world as well as for ourselves, we become part of the "priesthood of all believers".

Some time ago I took part in a local concert. While waiting for my cue I sat sidestage, knitting! I was dimly aware of a few irritated glances, but didn't realise how much I was in the way until the producer came up and said, in front of some of the others, "Would you move, please? It's a nuisance having you sitting there." The blood rushed to my cheeks as I gathered up my knitting and found a quiet corner to nurse my wounded pride.

A trivial event, certainly. But I felt, as I have never done before, what it is like to be unwanted in a particular place and told to go away. I found this bad enough, even though the producer had made a perfectly reasonable request. How, then, must it feel to be kicked around and told to "shove off" because of the colour of your skin? What must it be like to be an alcoholic sleeping rough on the street and constantly glared at by passing shoppers?

Because of the silly incident of the knitting, I now felt I could pray in a deeper way for the forgotten and marginalised people of the world. I had had a tiny taste of the inside story, and I could offer my hurt as a prayer for all refugees, and for those pushed out of their homes in South Africa, because the place where they lived was to become a "whites-only" area.

And I realised with shame my own indifference to the fate of such people.

Solidarity through weakness

Sometimes we feel helpless to do anything about the appalling problems of the world. We are up against such huge odds, that we wonder if our feeble efforts at prayer and action are any use at all. And if we ourselves are tired out, we are tempted to stop trying altogether.

We forget that our sense of weakness is itself a gift that

we can offer to God. This has dawned on me from my
small involvement with the campaigns of the Birmingham
clergyman, the Rev Dr Dick Rodgers, for the release of
several Russian Christians, including Irina Ratushinskaya,
the poetess, Alexander Ogorodnikov, who was imprisoned
for holding Christian discussion groups in his flat, and
other brave people.

At times I have felt deeply frustrated, because I feared
these Christians might never know that we were caring
and praying for them. "Why bother, then?" whispers the
tempter.

But I have come to realise that this very helplessness is
my common link with all prisoners of conscience and victims of disaster. None of us is the "strong one", dishing out
our charity and prayers from a superior level. Weakness is
something we share with them, and through this bond,
offered to Jesus, an energy of love is generated in prayer.

The former American Secretary of State, Mr Schultz,
made a statement to his own nation in 1987 concerning
the holding of hostages in Lebanon. "When an American
is kicked around," he said, "we are all kicked around." I
would prefer to say, "When *anybody* is kicked around we're
all kicked . . ." And, what is more, "When someone kicks
a prisoner, I do it, too."

We are all part of the blindness and selfishness of the
world; we all wound others, even if our weapons are words
rather than boots. So in prayer we can bring to God the
sinfulness of the world, because we are very much a part
of it. 'God chose what is foolish in the world to shame the
wise, God chose what is weak in the world to shame the
strong' (1 Corinthians 1:28).

We often underestimate the power of the Holy Spirit working through prayer. Irina Ratushinskaya was held in freezing conditions, but was literally warmed by the prayers, albeit halting and haphazard, of ordinary people like us. She writes:

> Believe me, it was often thus:
> In solitary cells, on winter nights,
> a sudden sense of joy and warmth
> And a resounding note of love . . .
> In the most fearful prison hour.[12]

* * *

Lord, let my sorrow and pain become part of your healing and redeeming of the world.

Energies Let Loose in the World

Chains of hurt are easy to identify. Less obvious, but just as real, are chains of healing. When we forgive, an energy of love and reconciliation is released into the world, which may have consequences far beyond our knowledge.

When we have been hurt there may well be a string of factors lying behind the incident which have nothing directly to do with us. Suppose the elderly Miss Jones goes to the dentist. When she is called from the waiting-room she is stiff and slow in standing up, and drops her gloves onto the floor. As she painfully bends down to pick them up, the dental nurse, Mrs Sharp, snaps, "We haven't got all day, you know."

Miss Jones naturally feels hurt. But what she does not know is that Nurse Sharp's husband came home drunk and foul-mouthed last night.

Mr Sharp had been drinking because he was depressed since becoming unemployed . . .

He had lost his job because of an injustice at work . . .

The person responsible had borne a grudge against Mr Sharp for many years . . .

And so one could go on, back and back, tracing factors that made one hurt lead to another.

So when Miss Jones walks home feeling miserable, she is being touched, though she does not realise it, by the universal human ills of unemployment, injustice and resentment.

Much of our unhappiness is the product of a similar chain of hurt. Recently I telephoned somebody who had just returned from a depressing conference about poverty in South America. Tired and drained as she was, it is not surprising that she snapped down the phone when I was absent-minded about something. So the hurt I felt was a tiny, indirect result of the injustice and misery in that sub-continent, and opened up for me a new way of praying for the poor of South America because I now had an indirect link with them.

Obviously it would be absurd to make an artificial analysis of every trivial upset, like, 'My wife is nagging me because her mother forced her to eat cabbage.' But when we are trying to pray through a hurtful incident, it can help to ponder what lies behind the event, and to remember that our reaction will have wide repercussions, contributing either to the hatred or to the healing of all human beings.

We are part of something far greater than we imagine. We affect other people all the time, simply by what we are. Any individual act of forgiving, however small, changes the world for the better. The archaic syndrome of "an eye for an eye" and "a life for a life" is only broken by Jesus's sort of loving, which absorbs the pain and allows God to transform it into the miracle of forgiveness.

* * *

I touch and am touched by people . . . Together, during the span of our lives, by loving or withholding love, we shall have created or destroyed something of humanity.

Prue Wilson[13]

You're Going to Get Hurt

If we take our Christian commitment seriously, pain is going to be an integral part of our calling. This is not to say that hurtful stress should be sought for its own sake; nor do self-conscious "martyrs" do anyone any good. Yet it does seem that tension and conflict, far from being unhelpful in the Christian life, are actually fundamental to it.

The heart of God's redeeming work is the Cross, the point where our evil and his love meet in unfathomable suffering. A good deal of prayer is about being there with God, in the pain.

Imagine you are the only Christian in your department at work, and frequently face scorn and gibes about your faith.

Or you work hard in a campaign dealing with long-term aid for famine victims, and find yourself accused of not caring enough about local charities.

Or some people in your church show nothing but contempt for traditions of worship that have meant a tremendous amount to you.

Or others in your church cling to past ways so strongly that any new initiatives are torn to bits, and dismissed as "change for change's sake".

Or you are minister of an inner-city church, and deeply concerned about the Christian's vocation to care about desperate and deprived people; but a small group in your congregation are wearing down your confidence by constant opposition and negativity.

The list could go on for ever.

When this sort of thing happens to us, we hate it. The hurt we feel is not only for ourselves, but also for the principles which are under attack. This is a natural reaction, and Jesus himself felt low on occasions: "What an unbelieving and perverse generation! How long shall I be with you? How long must I endure you?" (Mark 9:19).

But Jesus's way of looking at pain also helps us to cope positively with these hurtful tensions. "Blessed are you when men revile you and persecute you and utter all kinds of evil against you falsely on my account" (Matthew 5.5). "In the world you will have trouble; but be of good cheer, I have overcome the world" (John 16:33).

Jesus's utter faithfulness to God brought inevitable conflict. As soon as he started preaching, he aroused hostility and opposition. His family thought he was mad, and tried to stop him teaching (Mark 3:21). The scribes and Pharisees were filled with righteous indignation when he mixed with "disreputable" people and healed on the Sabbath. The hard-liners in the establishment wanted him dead as soon as he began to make people alive.

Betrayed, denied and abandoned by his disciples, Jesus trod a path of humiliation in the eyes of the world. And he invites us to join him on that path of vulnerability:

> Anyone who wishes to be a follower of mine must leave self behind; he must take up his cross and come with me (Mark 8:34, NEB).

We cannot avoid conflict with those who exploit others or abuse the natural world for the sake of financial gain. We are bound to be distressed by people's hard and unforgiving attitudes, by apathy outside the Church and judgmentalism within it. Prayer makes us more aware, and opens us up to what is going on around us. We become involved in the suffering of others, absorbing with Christ some of the barbs and blows with which human beings wound each other. To hunger and thirst for righteousness and peace may be blessed, but it is also costly.

We do not stand sinless in the middle of a world of sinners. But, as salt in a stew or leaven in a loaf, we do have a particular and demanding role as Christians among the people with whom we live.

We know this in theory. Most of us think we are ready to take up our cross and follow Christ. Yet, when the suffering comes, it is neither heroic nor glamorous, and we don't want it. Pain is pain, and we heartily wish that God would do something to rid us of this unpleasant experience as soon as possible. But the alternative is a safe cocoon of ignorance and loneliness. Saving our own life would be much easier; but at what cost?

> Whoever would save his life will lose it; and whoever loses his life for my sake and the gospel's will save it (Mark 8:21).

Not long ago I was at a prayer meeting for South Africa. Somebody had just read out a report about the way a black teenage boy had been reduced to a vegetable as a result of beatings and electric shocks from security police. In a time of free prayer that followed, a young man next to me was very distressed about the whole situation. He prayed, "Oh God, I feel so angry. I want revenge on the people who do these things. God forgive me."

And he wept.

The misery and shame of wanting revenge are sometimes a part of the suffering laid on us. We are part of the pain and evil of the world, and are shaken both by the highest and by the basest motives. It is by offering all of this to God in prayer that it can be redeemed, from the inside.

Two parables of discipleship

The following story is based on the experience of a friend. John (not his real name) goes to a party and someone says loudly, "I'm not a racist, but I can't bear all those black faces in the queue in front of me." John feels the blood rising to his cheeks, and plunges into a painful argument. Some people are exasperatingly flippant, while others express opinions based on sheer prejudice and wrong information. The host is embarrassed and tries to restore jollity by teasing John, "You Christians are such goody-goodies."

John goes home with a heavy heart, churning over people's apparent lack of sensitivity; he feels that he has made a mess of the whole business, and regrets that he didn't put certain points more convincingly.

Frustration of this sort is the cost of caring, and the cost of discipleship. The sheer offering to God of pain such as this is creative, even if there are no apparent "results."

There is another story, from the Philippines, about a fine bamboo tree which grew on a large estate. One day the owner came to cut it down. The bamboo begged to be spared, but to no avail. "You are needed for a water-pipe," he was told, "because there has been a drought."

So the bamboo agreed; but worse was to come. Each partition inside the joints in his huge, hollow stem had to be cut out. Again he protested. But when he saw the parched fields and half-starved families, he relented.

After he had been carved out as a channel of life-giving water for all those people, he was glad that he no longer stood secure and untouched in the plantation.

* * *

The stone which the builders rejected has become the corner-stone (Mark 12:10).

Lord Jesus, it is when you are most unwanted, kicked

around and useless in worldly terms, that you are most acutely and keenly present.

Watch Out!

When being a Christian becomes costly, the devil has a curious knack of creeping in. We may start congratulating ourselves for suffering more than other people, or begin believing that God thinks we are more virtuous than most.

Focusing on ourselves like this only narrows our vision, clogs up the channels of God's mercy and grace, and detracts from the value of anything we may have done for Christ anyway.

We all know people who never let us forget how much they have endured in a good cause. They sometimes reckon that they have a special right to lay down the law, as if their trials have given them some sort of unique contact with the Holy Spirit. Or else they expect permanent sympathy and concessions from everybody. It is easy to spot this happening in other people, but we do it too, if we are not careful: "I've been giving of myself to people all day; everyone ought to realise how tired I am and how hard I've been working . . ."

Jesus made short shrift of such attitudes in his parable about the hard-working slave (Luke 17.7–10, NEB).

Suppose one of you has a servant ploughing or minding sheep. When he comes back from the fields, will the master say, "Come along at once and sit down"? Will he not rather say, "Prepare my supper, fasten your belt, and then wait on me while I have my meal; you can have yours afterwards"? Is he grateful to the servant for carrying out his orders? So with you: When you have carried out all your orders, you should say, "We are servants and deserve no credit; we have only done our duty."

* * *

A good way to pray when we slip into self-satisfaction is to share our silliness with God, and picture ourselves standing on the pedestal that we seem to want, labelled:

SPECIAL CASE
THE CENTRE OF THE UNIVERSE

Weeping as Prayer

Frustration and misery about human suffering can sometimes drive us to tears; we feel so useless and without hope for any solution.
But the weeping can itself be offered as prayer.

A friend once told me how she had been deeply distressed about the famine in Africa, and had wanted to do all she could to respond to the need. At a meeting of her church council she had tried to raise the issue, but everyone was so preoccupied with organising a parish supper that there wasn't time. What enraged her most was that a great deal of energy had been thrown into arguments about table-decorations; people were dying of hunger while the debate raged over doilies.

She went home and wept in sheer frustration. The next day she sat down to pray, but wondered how she could do it because she was so depressed and churned up. But her pain and anger *were* her prayer at that moment for the starving people of the world. Her weeping was as important a part of her offering as her subsequent practical action.

Two other friends have told me how they wept over news items. One of them cried and prayed while the Zeebrugge ferry disaster was going on in 1987, and felt that God was drawing her to be deeply involved in the suffering there. Another friend found himself weeping at the murder of a whole family in Khartoum, whose children were the same age as his; again, he identified emotionally with them.

Clare Amos gives another graphic instance of how weeping can be intercession for those in great suffering. I quote at length:

> I was revisiting St George's Cathedral – the focal point of the Anglican Diocese of Jerusalem – where once I used to work . . . A group of us Westerners wanted to visit a Palestinian refugee camp. Jazalone was chosen, about 10–15 miles from Jerusalem . . .
>
> One of the party asked if we could see a refugee home. After some hesitation we were taken to visit a home which contained a woman with three small children around her. It was one room, no bigger than the average English lounge . . . We asked how many people lived

there. Fourteen. All in this one room? "Well," said the woman of the house, "we used to have three rooms. But the Israelis came and concreted over the entrance to the other two so that we can't use them."

The woman told us why. Her oldest son had been deported after he had finished a jail sentence for anti-Israeli activities. Her second son was currently in prison. The third boy was due to be sentenced . . .

After the woman had finished telling us all this, one of her three toddlers piped up – a boy of about five – "And when I grow up I'm going to go to prison too."

. . . That child's thoughtless remark seemed the most terrible thing of all. For he is perhaps right. Perhaps the hopelessness is the special horror of the Middle East, and of the conflict between Palestinians and Israelis. There is one land, and there are two peoples, both with a history of suffering, and who both claim it . . .

Is that boy also destined to become enmeshed in the cycle of violence – his powerless grey-black future compensated for only by the bitterness of his anger? And that woman, his mother, what must be her thoughts as she raises her children as fodder for Israeli jails? Hers is surely a hopelessness that few of us in England can begin to fathom . . .

We returned to Jerusalem, to the slightly faded but still secure bastion of St George's. And I wept. Wept from a sense of frustration laced with guilt. Guilt for having a comfortable home in Cambridge, guilt for the mess the British mandate had created in Palestine, frustration because I felt powerless and could do nothing . . .

And then I realised that perhaps in weeping I am in

fact doing something important. Weeping expresses my common humanity with Arab and Israeli that transcends our divisions. Somehow when we weep we express the fact that we can't control our world, or indeed our human existence, or life or death. We acknowledge our dependence and our powerlessness, but beyond that, our love . . .

"See how He must have loved him," they said of Jesus as they watched Him weeping for his dead friend, Lazarus. Weeping and love belong together. For the world's ultimate sanity men as well as women will have to learn how to weep . . .

And, in some mysterious way, tears can begin to lead to resurrection, they are agents of transformation. Only those that sow in tears are told that they shall reap in joy. We are promised that there will come a time when God will wipe away all tears from our eyes. But that is a promise even God cannot keep unless we first learn how to weep.[14]

* * *

When you weep,
You have a unique opportunity
To give this dark thing to God –
An offering from the inside of the shadow.

It is as if you bring the whole world with you.
This is the priesthood of all believers:
Christians in the mud with the rest,
Reaching out to God on behalf of us all;

And sharing the pain of creation with its Creator.

PART 2

Praying With Our Own Sinfulness

It is said that St Jerome, the great fourth-century biblical scholar, once said to Jesus in a dream, "Lord, what can I give to you? My money? My books? Or my learning?"

And the Lord replied, "Give me your sins; give me your desires."

Into the Sun and Wind of God

What are we to do with our selfishness and sin? It rarely works to make grand resolutions, telling ourselves that we will never again fall into familiar errors. We need instead to turn away from self-preoccupation, and focus our attention onto God, so that he can do the transforming work in us that we cannot do on our own.

There are all sorts of popular misconceptions about the prayer of penitence.

Some people imagine that we come to God full of guilt and dread, because he seems such a judgmental figure.

Others suppose that penitence is basically an academic exercise, working through a list of possible ways of breaking the Ten Commandments, and racking your brains to try and remember when you did so.

Or there is the well known caricature of the sacrament of Confession, by which you can sin as much as you like on Friday night, because the priest will automatically absolve you on Saturday morning. In that distortion, penitential prayer is nothing more than a sham.

We need another picture.

A parable at sea

I watched a family on the cross-Channel ferry from Folkstone to Boulogne. They were obviously on a holiday treat, a day-trip to France, and our ship would soon be setting sail.

Half an hour passed, and we still hadn't moved; one hour, and by now the children were restless and scratchy. Mum was harassed and trying vainly to amuse them, becoming increasingly irritable every time they asked, "When are we going?" Dad went off to join the bar-queue in disgust.

Eventually we left Folkstone. A little while later Dad came back, beer in hand, complaining, "Now we'll only have a short time in France before we have to come back again."

The children then began to squabble over who should read which comic. Eventually Mum declared, "Right. We're not going to have any more arguments today!"

They sank into a gloomy silence.

But gradually the scene was transformed. The sheer exhilaration of the sun and wind, the colours of the sea and the distant view of Dover's cliffs, combined to lift everyone out of their bad mood into something infinitely greater.

The children were the first to be affected. They stood at the rail, soaking up the sunshine and the smells and sound of the sea. Then Mum put down her newspaper, and they began to laugh together about seagulls perched in comical places on the mast. In the end Dad went and joined them as well.

It was as if the irritation and whining had been absorbed and dissolved in the refreshing breeze and movement of the sea-voyage. The family had found itself again, not because they had sat down and had a committee meeting about how to get on together, but because they had been swept up into something bigger than themselves. They had turned round, stood next to each other, and let themselves go into the sunshine.

I cannot count how many times I have said to myself, "I will never be irritable again," or, "I will not make any more thoughtless remarks." But it never works, and sooner or later I slip into the same old pitfalls once more. My mistake in these resolutions is to assume that I can overcome my sinfulness by my own efforts alone. I am forgetting that I also depend on God's grace.

Once we have realised and confessed our sins, it is best to turn away from ourselves to God, like the family on the ship turning their faces into the wind and sun. Then our love of God and desire to do his will can swallow up our petty selfishness, so that it begins to loosen its hold on us.

Concentrating on self-improvement only leads to despair.

Concentrating on God makes forgiveness and transformation possible.

Later on we may notice, with surprise, that changes are taking place in us after all.

* * *

"Behold," says the Lord, "I am doing a new thing, now it springs forth, do you not perceive it?
I, I am He
Who blots out your transgressions for my own sake,
and I will not remember your sins.

79

I have swept away your transgressions like a cloud,
and your sins like mist;
return to me, for I have redeemed you" (Isaiah 43:25; 44:22).

Let me open my eyes to the glory and the sunshine of God in his creation.

Let me open my heart to receive the full impact of his love.

Let his radiant fire burn away all that is rotten in me.

Let me breathe in the fresh air of life, on which I depend in the miracle of existence.

Let the wind of God's Spirit blow through me and clear away the cobwebs and rubbish.

I surrender my whole being to the wind and sun of God's love.

And we all, with unveiled face, beholding the glory of the Lord, are being changed into his likeness from one degree of glory to another (2 Corinthians 3:18).

What, No Struggle?

Just because grand resolutions to overcome our sins are seldom successful, this does not mean that we are excused from the fight against evil. We all have to struggle against a whole range of temptations and selfish impulses.

"Repenting" means literally "turning round", away from self

and towards God, for forgiveness and strength. This is where the main battle lies, because the pull of evil can be unnervingly strong.

How do you pray when you want to have an affair with somebody's husband or wife, or feel tempted to seize a subtle way of getting your own back on someone? Prayer seems almost impossible when our destructive emotions are at their highest.

If we try to repress our desires, we only become their slaves. A strong emotion is a fact which must be faced, however unpalatable; what matters is what we do with it. We have to open up our selfish inclinations to Christ, again and again if necessary, so that he can purge and purify them.

Wallowing in self-contempt is unhealthy, because it focuses our attention on ourselves. We do better to make a beeline for Jesus, and concentrate on the way he lived and taught. It is being with him that changes us. Jesus had a party with the tax-gatherers and ruffians of Capernaum *before* they began to examine their consciences!

And Levi made him a great feast in his house; and there was a large company of tax collectors and others sitting at table with them. And the Pharisees murmured, saying, "Why do you eat with tax collectors and sinners?" And Jesus answered them, "Those who are well have no need of a physician, but those who are sick; I have not come to call the righteous, but sinners to repentance." (Luke 5:29–30).

If there is a particular weakness that we often see in

ourselves, it is useful to have a specific phrase or prayer with which to confront it. For example, my weakness may be a desire always to avoid conflict; this temptation has to be met, not just by my telling myself to be braver, but by another weapon: words of Jesus such as, 'In the world you will have trouble. But be of good cheer, I have overcome the world' (John 16:33). Or when I wish I could be less irritable, I can use a prayer like 'Jesus, live in me', rather than simply nagging myself about keeping my mouth shut. Overcoming sin is a partnership with God, not a solo struggle.

Of course, we need to be aware of our faults, and of the effect our selfishness has on other people. But without the additional help of something greater than our own efforts to improve, we will not get very far.

* * *

We are justified by faith in Jesus Christ, and not by works of the law, because by works of the law shall no one be justified (Galatians 2:16).

A person who wishes to begin a good life should be like a man who draws a circle. Let him get the centre in the right place and keep it so and the circumference will be good. In other words, let a man first learn to fix his heart on God and then his good deeds will have virtue; but if a man's heart is unsteady even the great things he does will be of small advantage.

Meister Johannes Eckhart (1260–1327)

Am I centred, rooted and grounded in God? Everything I am and do springs from my centre. I will never overcome self just by cutting away its fruits; the roots need to be dealt with, by being plunged deep into God.

Guilt – Friend or Foe?

Guilt is meant to be a servant, not a master. Many people carry round a burden of unresolved guilt, which becomes a blockage to prayer, destroys self-respect and takes away inward peace.

If it is functioning properly, however, guilt puts itself out of a job.

Guilt has its place, and Christianity is not an excuse to brush off our sins as if they did not matter.

But guilt is also liable to get too big for its boots. If we are troubled by something we have done wrong, guilt can find a foothold inside us and wear down our morale, until we begin to imagine that we are beyond redemption. However many times we confess our sins to God, we never really feel that we are forgiven.

Destructive guilt needs to be turned on its head and transformed into the positive tool it was meant to be.

The very fact that we feel guilty is worth pondering. Why do we feel this way? Our shame must spring from a desire, deep inside us, to live honestly and lovingly, and to be reconciled with ourselves, other people and God. Otherwise we would never have started feeling guilty in the first place.

This desire for what is good and right is like a tiny flame, placed in us by God. We feel guilty because we know we have betrayed that flame. But guilt should also lead us to God's forgiveness so that we can be freed from our burden.

I vividly remember my first biology lesson at secondary school, when the teacher dissected a rat. I felt strangely shocked at the way this small creature was totally opened out and exposed to us; nothing inside him could be hidden from our gaze.

Some people with a burden of guilt think that prayer is going to be like that. They see religion as pointing an accusing finger at them, and fear some awful exposure or humiliation if they approach God.

Nothing could be further from the true Christian gospel. We are invited to repent, yes. But repentance is a freedom and a release. The primary message of Jesus, and the apostles after him, was simply, "Your sins are forgiven." The joyful, overwhelming and illogical fact of being totally forgiven *is* the gospel!

The only similarity between Christian prayer and the fate of the unfortunate rat is that there is no way we can hide the dark things in ourselves from God. But there is also a huge difference. When we allow God to open us up, we are not brutally dismembered or surrounded by curious, mocking stares. The only eyes gazing on us are the compassionate and gentle eyes of Christ. We will, of course, feel sad and ashamed when our puny sinfulness is laid bare to him. But there is nothing to fear.

We can never earn our salvation by our own efforts. Forgiveness is God's free gift, the outrageous miracle of undeserved mercy which he is waiting to offer us, if we will only turn in faith, however haltingly, and receive it. But if we refuse to open up, parts of us will remain cold and unhealed.

* * *

If you are feeling the pain of guilt, it is worth making space for a time of solitude with God (even if you can only find five or ten minutes), so that you can open it all up to him.

Expose your memories before God, without fear. Tell him everything. He is waiting to stretch out his arms to you.

Turn your face towards him in complete confidence. Allow his mercy and love to soak deeply into you.

Forget about the details of what you did wrong. Concentrate instead on the God who loves you.

Hear him say to you,

"I have relieved your shoulder of the burden;
In your distress you called, and I have delivered you"
(Psalm 81:6).

"You are my beloved child; my heart yearns for you, and I will surely have mercy on you" (Jeremiah 31:20).

"Your sins are forgiven" (Mark 2:5).

Music can feature in this sort of praying. There is a lovely melody by Grétry, the *Air de Ballet*, from the opera *Zémire et Azor*[1]. The plot is based on the fairy tale *Beauty and the Beast* and this section of the opera conveys the pure love of Beauty, which has the power to restore the beast to his real self. So this music is particularly appropriate when we are asking God to love and transform the beast in us into the person we were meant to be. It is especially helpful to read verses from the Bible (such as those quoted above) immediately before listening, or while the music is playing.

There are many other pieces of music which can enhance prayer in this way. Possibilities include:[2]

Bach: Double Violin Concerto, 2nd movement.

Bach: Concerto for Oboe and Strings, BWV 1060, 2nd movement.

Beethoven: Piano Concerto No 5 (Emperor), 2nd movement.

Some people are also helped by songs such as "Be Still and know that I am God" on *Come and Worship* with the choir of St Michael-le-Belfry, York[3], or "Breathe on Me" on *My Spirit Will Come*.[4]

The Stab of Remorse

Some of the most poignant scenes in plays occur when people who are feeling miserable are gently encouraged to turn their face towards a compassionate person. Praying with our sins is like that. God is not there to make us feel wretched; nor is he keeping us at arm's length. He is intimately close, waiting for us to turn and receive his forgiveness.

It is a horrible sensation when we realise that we have hurt somebody, especially a person we love. A flash of irritation, a thoughtless remark, or an over-harsh reprimand of the children, can give us a sharp stab of remorse afterwards. Even when we have apologised, they still feel the hurt, and we wish we could do more to put things right.

There is in fact something constructive we can do with the pain of remorse. We can face it and bear it *as a prayer for the people we have hurt.*

The desire to put things right by doing something specific is a natural instinct. On more than one occasion I have come home with a potted plant for my husband, after we have had a row! It helps to have a tangible object like this, as an outward sign of wanting to make amends.

But when it comes to putting things right between us and God, we cannot. The debt we owe him is so great, we could never "make it up" in a dozen lifetimes. Much of the elaborate Old Testament system of sacrifices was an expression of this fundamental longing to set things right between us and God. But the startling news that Jesus brought is that God does not require this. Like the father of the prodigal son, God simply waits to come towards us and embrace us when we turn back to him.

The son in that parable badly wanted to prove how sorry he was. He had it all worked out, and had planned to say to his father: "I am no longer worthy to be called your son; treat me as one of your hired servants."

But all he got for his pains was an enormous hug; before he could finish his penitential speech, his delighted father was instructing the servants: "Bring quickly the best robe . . . put a ring on his hand and shoes on his feet . . . let us eat and make merry . . ." (Luke 15:18–25).

On the cross, Jesus's sacrifice was the final putting-right of our alienation from God. He absorbed all our human sinfulness in an act of total self-annihilation, and transformed it into the marvellous energy of resurrection-madness which swept through the first-century apostles – madness, at least, in the eyes of the world. Jesus has saved us from the destructive power of guilt, as well as from the frightening dead-end of having to rely on ourselves alone.

The Cross is beyond time. There is no evil that Jesus has not entered into; no rift between us and God that he has not bridged; and no wrong that he has not received into himself and overcome.

If Jesus has done all this for us, what is required on our part? Only that we should turn towards him in complete honesty, as we face the painful knowledge of our persistent betrayal of what we know to be right.

One of the most crucial verses in the Old Testament comes in Isaiah 30:15: "In returning [lit. *turning*] and rest you shall be saved; in quietness and in trust shall be your strength."

Turn ... return ... turn again ... in quietness and stillness – this is Jesus's invitation too, in the lifelong process of conversion.

The miracle of salvation is that we can say "Yes" to God, even when we still have so much self-centredness, greed and unkindness in our nature. He doesn't rub our noses in the mud, but instead offers us his unconditional embrace.

* * *

Love bade me welcome: yet my soul drew back,
   Guiltie of dust and sinne,
But quick-ey'd Love, observing me grow slack
   From my first entrance in,
Drew nearer to me, sweetly questioning,
   If I lack'd any thing.

A guest, I answer'd, worthy to be here:
   Love said, you shall be he.
I the unkinde, ungratefull? Ah my deare,
   I cannot look on thee.
Love took my hand, and smiling did reply.
   Who made the eyes but I?

Truth Lord, but I have marr'd them: let my shame
   Go where it doth deserve.
And know you not, sayes Love, who bore the blame?
   My deare, then I will serve.
You must sit down, sayes Love, and taste my meat:
   So I did sit and eat.

George Herbert (1593–1633)[5]

Jesus was left alone with the woman taken in adultery. He looked up and said to her, "Where are they? Has no one condemned you?" She said, "No one, Lord." And Jesus said, "Neither do I condemn you; go, and do not sin again" (John 8: 10–11).

Self-protection

Self-protection underlies much of our sinfulness. When we are busy shielding ourselves, we slip all too easily into dishonesty and disloyalty; or else we build up defensive barriers which make us behave unkindly to other people.

At the painful moment when we realise that we have let God and our friends down like this, there is no escaping the consequences. We long for relief, but the truth has to be faced. The very fact that we feel wretched is a sign of hope, because it shows that we do want to be true and compassionate people, deep down.

In prayer Jesus draws out of us this desire to love.

Peter knew all about self-protection. That is what made him deny his Master.

Jesus had been arrested and dragged from one interrogation to another all night. The terrified disciples had fled, and Peter was now restlessly hanging around in the courtyard of the High Priest's house.

A servant-girl stared hard and challenged him: "*You're one of that man's followers, aren't you!*"

In a moment of sheer panic, Peter, who had loved and stuck by Jesus for so long, blurted out, "What the hell are you talking about? I tell you I don't know him."

Three times Peter denied all knowledge of Jesus. And then the cock crowed, and Peter rushed out and wept bitterly (Mark 14:53–72).

Most of us would have done the same.

We already do, in our own way. We are quick to make excuses for ourselves, often at the expense of other people. And we don't mind hearing criticisms about others, because we are relieved to find a scapegoat, even when we know that remarks being made are unjust.

How can we prevent this selfishness from spoiling our better nature? I am not sure that we can, on our own. But the way Jesus handled Peter gives us a clue as to how he deals with us when our self-protective instinct has been to the fore.

Do you love me?

During those days immediately after the crucifixion, Peter must have carried an intolerable burden of guilt. He must have longed to show Jesus how desperately he regretted his cowardice. But there seemed to be no way of putting things right. Restless and miserable, he thought he might find relief by doing something practical. So he went fishing with a few other disciples on the Sea of Galilee.

The story is familiar (John 21). They caught nothing all night. Then they saw the figure of Jesus standing on the shore, and he suggested that they cast their net on the other side of the boat. The haul of fish was massive.

Peter suddenly recognised Jesus, and leapt joyfully into the water, swimming to the shore.

And then, when the two men were face to face once more, it was Jesus who took the initiative in healing the guilt which was devouring Peter.

Peter had denied Jesus three times. So three times Jesus asked him, "Do you love me?"

In the first two questions Jesus used the ordinary word for human friendship: "Are you fond of me?"

The last time, Jesus asked Peter if he loved with the selfless love that is closest to the love of God. (The English translation hides the different Greek words for "love".)

Gradually Peter was able to come back to the truth about himself; beneath his surface desire to protect himself, he did indeed want to love and serve Christ.

Jesus had not said, "Peter, are you ever going to deny me again?" Instead he had asked the fundamental question: "Do you love me? What is your highest and best desire? Which way are you pulling – with me or against me?"

This is how Jesus handles us if we will let him. Our hope does not lie primarily in our own determination to mend our ways, but in our response to his simple question: "*Do you love me?*"

* * *

As the life of Christ takes hold on us, our lives will be transformed from being lives of self-protection, self-care, self-cultivation, into lives given for others, because God, the God of compassion, will have taken possession of our being. . . .

Gerard Hughes[6]

Jealousy

> "*O, beware, my lord, of jealousy;*
> *It is the green-eyed monster which doth mock*
> *The meat it feeds on.*"[7]

"I'm not a jealous person," we like to say to ourselves. That is probably true, in as much as we do not begrudge pop stars their fame or professors their brains, nor are we aching to be multi-millionaires. But we all have within us seeds of jealousy which occasionally come to the surface.

We can feel threatened by a person whose work is similar to ours, who is attractive, about the same age as us, and appears to be more successful than we are. We don't like it when a colleague gets a senior post which we had fancied for ourselves, and we are jealous of people who seem to be more popular, or receive more invitations to parties than we do.

It is a rare individual who will not wince inwardly when adverse comparisons are made:

"Mum, I wish *you* made cakes like this!" says the eldest child, amidst a chorus of agreement.

Or the newly-retired captain of a sports club overhears someone remarking in the bar: "This new lad, Ted, is the best captain we've had for years."

To our shame, most of us feel better when unfavourable things are said about the person we envy. Both the mother and the rugby player would probably be glad if someone else were to pipe up, "I don't agree! Mrs X's cakes are horrible!" or, "Maybe, but Ted is not as experienced as I would like."

I have tried various ways of praying through my feelings about somebody I envy. I know that, in my heart of hearts, I wish her no harm. So when I pray, I ask God to enable my better and deeper desire – for her good – to come to the surface, and swallow up my petty selfishness.

One exercise I have used is a bit gruesome, but it works. I ask myself what would happen if I heard that she had been badly injured in a car crash, or if something cruel had been written about her in a tabloid newspaper. Then I picture going to see her, and imagine how I would find her and how I would react. And I know that my concern at that moment would override any jealousy I might have felt. This helps me to pray for her in a more genuine and caring way.

My children once had a story book about a monster who terrorised a family, until a little boy drew a pencil picture of it and then rubbed it out. Exit monster!

Jealousy is like an ugly monster who blunders around inside us, trampling on our desire for other people to blossom, and spewing out purple smoke which forms the word "self" in the air.

It can be fun, and quite useful too, to draw a picture of our own Monster Jealousy when praying. But what about rubbing it out? It's not as easy to get rid of jealousy as it is to erase a pencil-sketch.

The best way is to pray for the person we envy, faithfully and regularly. We cannot genuinely intercede for somebody and simply dismiss them at the same time. Eventually we may find that the monster has disappeared. Or perhaps it has turned into something else.

* * *

Who can know his own unwitting sins?
O cleanse me from my secret faults (Psalm 19:12).

Purge me with hyssop and I shall be clean,
wash me and I shall be whiter than snow.
Create in me a clean heart, O God,
*   and renew a right spirit within me (Psalm 51:7, 10).*

What Do I Want?

We are all full of conflicting desires. We want to be generous, but we can be greedy and extravagant; we want to care about others, yet we put our own concerns first; we agree that we should stand up for what is right, yet we slip into compromises to make life easier for ourselves; we would hope to be peacemakers, yet we easily hurt people back.

*   Fortunately the matter does not end there. Our motley collection of desires is not a fixed or unchangeable part of our nature. Prayer gives God an opening, so that, through his work in us, our highest and best desires can have a bit more say in the way we live.*

I was watching my small son. It was the last day of November, and there on the wall was an unopened Advent calendar, sparkling with glitter, every door a tantalising mystery.

He touched a window above the stable and felt its edges. Yet something held him back from actually opening it. Though itching to peep at the picture beneath, he also wanted to save the delight for the right day. He knew from past experience that you spoil your own fun by cheating with an Advent calendar.

So he decided to wait. Conflicting desires had been pulling him in opposite directions, but the deeper urge, to save the excitement for the proper moment, had prevailed. He had stopped and given himself a chance to think out what mattered most.

Phyllis Bottome once wrote, "You are not free until your long desires are stronger than your short ones."[8] I find this a most penetrating remark. The term "short desires" suggests the things which clamour under our noses, to be quickly taken up in a selfish impulse; but a "long desire" conveys something more thoughtful, linked with ideals which have touched us at the spiritual high points in our lives.

Our daydreams teach us a lot about our "short desires", because they whisk us into all sorts of adventures in which we usually play a flattering role, often at the expense of other people. It is alarming how easily our integrity can be suspended in these daydreams, before we realise what we are doing.

Involuntary fantasies reveal many things which need to be laid open to God and purified. But how can we enable this to take place?

Recognising our desires

It is important to tell God exactly what we want, and not what we think we ought to want. Nothing blocks the channels of communion with God more efficiently than pious self-deception. If we are honest, he can do something with us. Having put our selfish desires into words, it is a useful exercise to take them to their logical conclusion. Suppose we do want possessions, or power, or somebody else's marriage-partner. What would happen if God always let us have our own way? Who would get hurt? What would we want next? What sort of person would we become?

What matters most to us?

Buried treasure

Jesus said, "The kingdom of heaven is like treasure hidden in a field, which a man found and covered up; then in his joy he goes and sells all that he has, and buys that field" (Matthew 13:44). We do have grounds for hope that our better and deeper desires will prevail over our superficial ones, not because we are virtuous Christians, but because God is at work in us.

If we ask ourselves, "What do I want to be the most important thing in my life?" it may be that, in the end, we would say, "The love of God." If so, that is a discovery of buried treasure which was put in us by God in the first place. We can confidently trust him to nurture and rekindle this desire for his love, when we ask that our "shorter" desires may be taken over and absorbed by our "longer" ones.

* * *

You know better than I how much I love you, Lord. You know it and I know it not, for nothing is more hidden from me than the depths of my own heart.

I desire to love you; I fear that I do not love you enough.
I beseech you to grant me the fulness of pure love.

Behold my desire; you have given it to me. Behold in your creature what you have placed there. O God, you love me enough to inspire me to love you for ever; behold not my sins. Behold your mercy and my love.

François Fénelon (1651–1715)

Lord, save me from being divided against myself. Let my will, inch by inch, become more completely yours.

Praying with Ambition

Ambitious musings can slither craftily into our stream of consciousness, and reveal all sorts of hidden longings to exalt our own ego. Translating our selfish desires literally into prayer helps to put them in a different perspective.

Not all ambition is wrong. There is nothing to be ashamed of in hoping for promotion or aiming to do great things.

The ambition which harms us is the sort which inflates our self-esteem out of all proportion . . .

"If I were to be chosen for this position of honour, awarded such and such a prize . . . reckoned to be the best . . . noticed by important people . . ."

Thus our egocentricity rattles on. We would be highly embarrassed if our idle thoughts were made audible to the outside world.

Selfish ambitions also distort the way we see other people. We start looking at them as useful cogs in our self-centred plans, or as threats to our cherished aims, rather than as fellow human-beings.

There is little point in declaring that we will never indulge in such thoughts again; we know ourselves too well. Nor can most of us honestly pray, "Lord, please put me at the bottom of every pile, to be neglected and trodden on by all."

An indirect attack is much more effective. See how it sounds if you make your ambition into an imaginary joke-prayer: "Dear Lord, I want to be elected onto the top committee, and I trust you will make everyone notice my skills. Keep all other candidates out of the limelight, O God, and silence those who know about my weaknesses, so that all people will acknowledge my superiority and vote accordingly. Amen."

Such a travesty of true prayer helps us to laugh with God about ourselves, and cut our ambition down to size. Maybe we can then move on to pray wholeheartedly, "Lord, I depend on you for my very existence, my skills, my experience, everything. And yet I am wanting prestige and power for myself. Show me what really matters, and let my longer and better desires overtake my short ones!"

Being pulled by ambitious thoughts is not the same as behaving ambitiously. It is encouraging to remember that even Jesus was tempted with thoughts of ambition, when Satan offered him "all the kingdoms and the glory of the world" (Matthew 4:8). But Jesus chose a way of humiliation instead of a path of glory.

The crucified figure is not there to bully us into self-loathing. Love, not retribution, pours down from the Cross. Yet there is a place for pondering the depth of suffering and degradation to which Jesus was prepared to go for our sake, when our own ambitions are riding high.

* * *

When I survey the wondrous cross,
On which the Prince of glory died,
My richest gain I count but loss,
And pour contempt on all my pride.

Isaac Watts (1674–1748)

Have this mind among yourselves, which you have in Christ Jesus, who, though he was in the form of God, did not count equality with God a thing to be grasped, but emptied himself, taking the form of a servant . . . and humbled himself and became obedient unto death, even death on a cross. (Philippians 2:5–8).

The Garden Path of Pride

Pride is one big hoax. It is plausible, because there is usually some truth in the evidence on which we congratulate ourselves, and it is dangerous, because we fail to see it. Lust you can't miss; anger you cannot avoid. But pride disguises itself as "moral superiority" or "spiritual maturity", so that before very long we have put on the Pharisee's distorting spectacles and thanked God that we are not like everyone else (Luke 18:11).

Pride is a cunning animal. It takes half the truth about ourselves, and makes it look like the whole truth.

"You have a lot of boots," James murmured.

"I have a lot of legs," the Centipede answered proudly, "and a lot of feet. One hundred, to be exact."

"*There* he goes again!" the Earthworm cried, speaking for the first time. "He simply cannot stop telling lies about his legs! He doesn't have anything *like* a hundred of them! He's only got forty-two! The trouble is that most people don't bother to count them. They just take his word. And anyway, there is nothing *marvellous*, you know, Centipede, about having a lot of legs."

"Poor fellow," the Centipede said, whispering in James's ear. "He's blind. He can't see how splendid I look."

"In my opinion," the Earthworm said, "the *really* marvellous thing is to have no legs at all, and to be able to walk just the same."

"You call that *walking!*" cried the Centipede. "You're a *slitherer*, that's all you are!"[9]

Pride also makes us greedy. We want to keep to ourselves all the praise we receive for doing things well, instead of passing it on to God. So we become more and more blown up with our own importance.

One way to pray with pride is to use a method I have mentioned earlier: putting what we are thinking into words, so that we see clearly how daft we are: "I really think I am much more advanced spiritually than most . . ." Or, "I am truly generous; other people are so uncommitted!"

Back to the Pharisee again!

But God takes us by surprise in the way he responds to our bursts of self-congratulation. He doesn't say, "Be quiet, you fool.' He enjoys with us the fact that something has gone well. But then he says to us, "This thing you're good at – haven't you noticed that it's mine as well as yours, a gift? If you're not careful, you'll damage it by clutching it so tightly. And you won't leave any room for me to do my work in you, if you are so cluttered up with your own achievements. Let go a bit!"

When we see how we have been filling ourselves with pride, we become free to send the credit and acclaim straight up to God. It is a relief to have no super cardboard image of ourselves to defend any more. We need no longer be afraid of criticism or of making mistakes – at least for the moment. . . . Pride has a way of creeping back on us unawares.

Humility is an elusive virtue, because as soon as we

think we've got it, we've lost it. If we don't know whether we are humble or not, that's a good sign!

* * *

The things that we love tell us what we are.
Thomas Merton[10]

O Lord you have searched me out and known me:
    you know when I sit or when I stand,
You comprehend my thoughts long before:
    you are acquainted with all my ways . . .
Such knowledge is too wonderful for me:
    so high that I cannot endure it . . .
Search me out, O God, and know my heart:
    put me to the proof and know my thoughts.
Look well lest there be any way of wickedness in me:
    and lead me in the way that is everlasting
                    (Psalm 139:1–2, 5, 23–24).

Self-consciousness

Trying to live a "good Christian life" is not without its hazards. One is pride; another is self-consciousness.

Paradoxically, we are more likely to become the person God wants us to be when we forget about our own "spiritual progress" altogether.

The unfortunate centipede is the object of much ridicule.

As well as Roald Dahl's portrayal of him as a conceited twerp, there is also a tale about a centipede who was perfectly mobile until someone asked him how he managed to walk with so many legs. As soon as he thought about which leg came after which, he began to trip himself up.[11]

A similar danger besets prayer. Trying to live prayerfully throughout the day can make us so self-conscious about every thought, word and mouthful, that we lose our vision of God. We will find him more readily by losing ourselves in our surroundings than by analysing our every response to those surroundings. An incident which I experienced in a cowshed might illustrate this.

During a family holiday some years ago, we were pottering around a farm. My children wanted to watch the cows being milked, and the farmer agreed, on condition that we stood completely still and quiet; a disturbance might stop the cows letting down their milk. We stood in a line at one end of the milking parlour, rapt in silent attention.

"This is just right for prayer," I thought to myself, and I began to concentrate on inner quiet so that I could "bring" prayer (as I thought) into this pastoral setting. While I was so busy trying to be holy, my eye fell onto a notice pinned on the wall behind a large black and white cow: "Careful! Number 16 kicks when tickled."

Laughing to myself, I realised how absurd my self-conscious effort to pray had been, as if I could make this scene prayerful by my own spiritual techniques. What I had to do was watch the activity around me, listen to the cows, smell the smells, and relish this splendid corner of Dorset with God.

We will not become a helpful, thoughtful member of the

family by telling ourselves a dozen times a day, "I am about to be a helpful, thoughtful member of the family." It will more likely happen when we forget ourselves and listen to the people we are so anxious to help!

Self-consciousness can cling to us like sticky treacle, but it melts of its own accord if we can turn our attention towards God and his world – and enjoy the cows, or whatever comes our way!

* * *

The quest of the self which God has meant each of us to be, is like the quest of happiness (which is indeed much the same thing) – it is not found by looking for it.

Austin Farrar[12]

The Same Old Sins

Sometimes we wonder when we will ever stop committing the same old sins. In this we are in good company: "I do not do the good I want," wrote St Paul, "but the evil I do not want is what I do" (Romans 7:19).

The cock didn't stop crowing the day Peter denied Christ, either for him or for us. Redemption is a long, slow process, and the closer we come to God, the more deeply we dig into ourselves, finding layers of rottenness we had not known were there.

It is a blow to our pride, apart from anything else, to find that we have fallen into the same old failures yet again.

Maybe we thought we were getting beyond such things. Or at least we hoped that God was changing us for the better.

He probably was – but not in the way we expected. Often the transforming work we have asked him to do leads us into chastening experiences we hadn't bargained for. Instead of being wonderfully freed from all selfish desires, we find deeply-rooted sins coming to the surface, which need to be confessed again and again. Reluctantly we admit that we are not the ideal creatures we would like to think we are.

But we can take heart. The very fact that we are looking for God and trying to follow his way means that we have, in a sense, found him. We do not have to pass a test of moral virtue before we can be close to him.

The journey towards God is a spiral, not a straight line. We are not presented with a list of sins, to be ticked off one by one, in a steady progress leading to perfection. We will inevitably encounter the same weaknesses and commit the same, wretched sins as time goes on. But we are a slightly different person each time it happens. Whenever we confess our repeated failures to God, his love penetrates a fraction more deeply into us.

We naturally feel disheartened that we continue to let God down. But this should not stop us trying. Each mistake healed and forgiven is a step towards union with Christ, even though we cannot see much progress ourselves.

Imagine the opposite of our situation. Someone has a dramatic Christian conversion experience, and assumes that he has "made it" spiritually, not realising that this is a beginning rather than an end. What happens? Perhaps he is so discouraged when he sees that he is still liable to weaknesses, that he gives up the whole business as a hoax. Or else he develops a false complacency ("I'm okay; I've made my decision for Christ, so I don't have to worry now") and settles down into a mediocre discipleship with neither pain nor growth. In such a person the hidden, selfish motives and buried resentments would remain untouched and therefore unhealed.

This is not to say that being a sinful Christian is a good thing! Paul faced a similar distortion of his teaching when some people from Rome challenged him: "Are we to continue in sin that grace may abound?" (Romans 6:1). Of course not!

But God can work *through* the chaos of our human failures, to bring new goodness that we would never have imagined. It is right that our sinfulness should distress us. Sin damages other people and ourselves only too clearly. But at the same time, we can grow through our errors, if we ask God to teach us more about ourselves, purify our desires, and make us more dependent on Him.

When offered to God, the mess of our life is redeemed.

* * *

A Prayer with a Candle

My Lord and my God –
thank you for drawing me to Yourself . . .
Lord,
You have told us that the pure in heart shall see God
– the single-minded

who do not try to serve two masters,
who have no other gods but You.
Keep the burning of my desire for you
as clear and steady as the flame of a candle
– a single, undivided focus of attention,
a steady offering of the will.
Let my whole being be filled with Your light
so that others may be drawn to You.
Let my whole being be cleansed by the flame of Your love
from all that is contrary to Your will for me,
from all that keeps others from coming to You.
Let my whole being be consumed in Your service,
so that others may know Your love,
– my Lord and my God.

Margaret Dewey[13]

Forgiveness – A Choice

Being forgiven is not like visiting the dentist for a filling so that
we can chew again unaided; nor is it like a garage-repair, fixing
our car so that it can run under its own steam.

Forgiveness is a process which we need all the time, not only
to cleanse us from past sins, but also to make us more the person
we are meant to be – in God's image. This is what salvation is
about.

I often wonder what had been going on inside Zacchaeus,
the unpopular little tax-man from Jericho, before he met

Jesus (Luke 19:1–10). Perhaps he had already begun to wish he could shake himself free from the web of double-dealing and deceit in which he was trapped. If he refused to support the Roman government, he would lose his job; he must feed his family! If he stopped cheating, everyone would assume he had some ulterior motive. And to admit to the slippery tactics used by all tax-collectors would lose him the last few friends he had in the trade.

Maybe he longed, underneath it all, to live generously and openly, and find real friendship and trust. Smatterings of Jesus's teachings must have circulated around Jericho. And now Jesus was approaching, and Zacchaeus wanted to get a bit closer to this figure whose ideas drew him like a magnet, in spite of himself.

So the drama begins, in the familiar story of Zacchaeus sitting in a sycamore tree, well hidden (as he thinks) from the ridicule of the neighbours. Then Jesus astonishes everyone by stopping and looking up: "Zacchaeus, I'm going to have dinner with *you* today!"

We can hardly imagine Zacchaeus's mixed reaction of delight and embarrassment at this moment. And then the joy and exhilaration when he finds the freedom to give back four times the value of what he has extorted from people, and to share the rest of his wealth extremely generously.

Now he no longer depends on worldly security or reputation. He has found something infinitely more valuable. And all this has happened because he opened his door to Jesus, who accepted and loved him *as he was*. This is what enabled Zacchaeus to discover his real self.

There are many ways of praying with this story. One is to use the imagination.

Be Zacchaeus; climb a tree and hope nobody sees you. Watch Jesus walking towards your tree; watch him looking up at you, and see all the crowds staring at you too. Listen to Jesus inviting himself to your house. Let him come home and sit down with you. What happens next?

Or you can ponder the way Jesus dealt with Zacchaeus. He didn't come storming into Zacchaeus's house, banging on the door and sweeping in with a tirade of condemnation. He waited until Zacchaeus had freely chosen to look out for him. He entered his house as a guest. And he transformed Zacchaeus by sitting down and eating with him.

If we were forced to love God, it would not be love. God enables us to give him our own free and generous response.

*   *   *

Lord, I know You take me as I am;
but I want You to make me
what You would have me to be.
                    Richard Harries[14]

"Behold I stand at the door and knock; if any one hears my voice and opens the door, I will come in to him and eat with him, and he with me" (Revelation 3:20).

You're Not Going to Keep Your Hands Clean

Christians are not sinless mortals floating round in an otherwise sinful world. We share the fallen human condition, and bear a corporate responsibility for the apathy and cruelty which damage so many people.

We are called, not only to serve Christ by standing up for what is right and loving, but also to bring to God the mess and muddle of the world of which we are a part.

It is not easy to be a Christian in an environment where people's standards and values are very different from your own. I heard recently about someone – I shall call her Jan – whose husband's firm treated several employees and their spouses to a weekend in a luxury hotel. Jan is somebody who thoroughly enjoys life and loves a treat. But there was something about this weekend that sickened her.

She is a committed Christian, deeply involved in working for famine relief, and part of a hospital chaplaincy team. Her whole life is geared to finding ways of giving hope to distressed and underprivileged people.

On this weekend she suddenly found herself in a glut of luxury upon luxury, and she felt miserable at the way other members of the party seemed to complain more than enjoy the experience. She could not shake off a feeling of waste and extravagance, but then chided herself for being judgmental.

Her main sensation was loneliness, because everyone

seemed so preoccupied with things that were unimportant to her. At one level she and her husband belonged to that world, but, at another, they did not. She did not want to be a kill-joy or take a puritanical stance against everyone else. Yet she wondered if her silence was somehow compromising her belief that luxury is a treat, not a right, and that the good things of the world are enjoyed by sharing and not by grasping.

Many Christians face a similar dilemma, finding themselves in a tough, competitive world in which certain fundamental values are different from their own. This is not to say that business and industry are evil in themselves, or that it is wrong to make a profit! But difficult questions arise if you have to work in a situation where financial gain is given higher priority than human safety; or where your firm exploits those who are desperate for jobs, by forcing them to work very long hours and threatening redundancy if they refuse.

How is a Christian to cope with this kind of situation? Many would like to pull out altogether, feeling that they are compromising their standards simply by being part of that world.

Yet none of us will ever escape to a "perfect Christian environment". We are not going to keep our hands clean. Our calling is to be in the world, even if not of it. And that often means sticking it out where we are, not turning a blind eye to corruption, but praying like mad for the discernment to know when to speak out, and when simply to be there, as Christ's leaven in the dough.

Jan's uncomfortable feeling in a velvety hotel lounge is a parable of the tension facing all Christians. As the author of the Letter to the Hebrews says, "Here we have no permanent home, but we are seekers after the city which is to come" (1:14 *NEB*). We belong to two worlds at once, and this is a tension which we cannot avoid. We share the sinful condition of all human beings. But we have been touched by a vision of something else, the joyful simplicity and generosity of Christ.

The answer is not to escape from one world into the other, but to remain uncomfortably in both, though prepared to face the cost when loyalty to God makes conflict with our fellows inevitable.

When we allow our anger or bitterness to hurt other people, we are adding to the destructive energy which leads to violence and war in the world. When we look at the pollution of the earth and the plight of the starving, we must remember that there is in each one of us a small part of the blindness, greed and selfishness which cause these things on a global scale.

So we need to expose to God the evil in ourselves, not only for personal forgiveness, but also as prayer for the healing of our violent and ravaged world.

In her booklet *Creative Suffering*[15], Iulia de Beausobre talks about a traditional Russian Christian figure, the "holy fool", whose vocation is to mix with the outcasts of society. He lives with rogues and eats with beggars, so that he can participate in their life, and offer it to Christ for healing and redemption *from the inside*. This, too, could become a parable for us.

In the days when I took my young children to school, the early morning rush was often fraught with irritability and impatience, as everyone charged around hunting for library books and swimming things, falling over each other in the process. I remember on more than one occasion being sharp with my youngest for dancing round under my feet when I was trying to get everyone organised. After taking them to school, I would come home heavy-hearted at having given the children such a bad start to the day, and annoyed with myself for being so thoroughly bad-tempered.

It was reassuring to talk to other young mums, and discover that their early mornings were often the same. Familiar themes kept coming up: tiredness, frustration at the seeming impossibility of ever getting organised; anxiety about the children's day; and annoyance when people didn't immediately do as they were told!

Shake all these ingredients together in a busy parent on a rushed morning, and – POP – the cork will fly out. But we can pray for each other from the middle of the tears and the mess, because we are all in the same boat.

* * *

Abba Father,
With You, in my sinfulness,
   Offering the world.
With You in my weariness,
   Offering the world.
With You in my need of You,
   Offering the world.
With You in unbounded trust,
   Offering the world.

From Self to Silence

Silence can be an effective weapon against our sinfulness. When we are before God in the stillness, we have no words behind which to hide. Because we are empty-handed and exposed, the Holy Spirit can penetrate the deepest parts of our conscious and unconscious selves.

Self is very noisy: greed and ambition clamour for attention; temptations clatter away; resentment rattles on. Part of praying is letting this noise out into the hands of God, rather than just allowing it to bang around inside us. But then God offers a gift of silence, in which our hearts and wills can be purified.

An experienced teacher-friend tells me that one of the best ways to calm and quieten a class of young children is to speak softly. Then they all strain to hear, and settle down as a result. We can apply the same method to our jangling selfishness. Listen! God is whispering your name and saying, *Be still, and know that I am God* (Psalm 46:10).

When we become quiet with God, he touches the roots of our desires and actions. In the stillness we can lay ourselves open to be transformed by his all-pervading mercy and love. This has more effect on our sinfulness than a score of loud reprimands.

A way to become still

Sit in a comfortable but not floppy chair.

Say slowly and thoughtfully the first two verses of Psalm 63:

> O God, you are my God:
>   early will I seek you.
> My soul thirsts for you, my flesh longs for you:
>   in a dry and thirsty land where no water is.

Say it again. Then take out from this a few key words:

> O God, you are my God . . .
> My soul longs for You . . .

Repeat these phrases several times, until you feel that they are becoming part of you, sinking from your head to your heart like water into a dry plant.

> O God, you are my God
> My soul longs for you . . .

When you are ready, let the prayer become even shorter: *My God*, or, simply, *God*.

Let yourself go into the silence, using the name of God to draw you again and again into his presence which is beyond words.

When distractions come (which they will), offer them to God and then let go of them, returning to the full verse or to the simpler words, so that they can lead you back into a silent communion with God. Numerous passages from the Bible can be prayed with in this way.[16]

* * *

We seek "a laying aside of thoughts, a progressive self-emptying, a self-noughting, that we may be filled with an all-embracing sense of the Divine indwelling. He must increase but I must decrease . . .

. *Bishop Kallistos Ware*[17]

Silence . . . prepares the way for the union of the soul with the will of God.
Rule of the Society of the Love of God[18]

Distractions in Prayer

When a prayer-time has been invaded by buzzing thoughts about everything under the sun, we feel annoyed with ourselves for letting in so much clutter. We may be tempted to give up praying altogether and leave it to the "experts". But this would be a sad mistake. Everyone has distractions. Instead of letting them destroy our confidence, we should take hold of them, and then hand them over to God.

You are not a failure at prayer if you find yourself daydreaming about last night's television programme or tomorrow's meetings during a quiet time with God. You are normal. What matters is that you have made space to be with God in the first place, and that you genuinely *want* to give him all your attention. That desire counts more than anything else.

That is not to say that distractions are to be encouraged. I am thinking about the times when we are trying to keep our attention on God, and are having problems doing so.

There are, of course, many different kinds of distraction.

if we are overwhelmed by some great worry or unhappiness, that is bound to dominate our awareness during prayer. The main point of this book has been to explore how we can bring such troubles into our praying, rather than trying to pray *in spite of* them.

But at other times a welter of minor concerns bombards our minds. The vital moment is when we realise that we have wandered away from concentrating on God. A distraction is only sinful if at this point we deliberately continue it for our own pleasure, because to do that is to put other things before God.

So what do we do with our chatterbox minds?

Some would say that distractions should be banished by sheer willpower. I do not like that approach, first because suppressed thoughts tend to recur in any case, and secondly because this method drives our distractions away from God, as if there were certain areas in life outside the orbit of his concern.

I find that it is best to make the distraction into a prayer, by turning my face back to God, and bringing with me the thing that had come to mind. It is like turning round to face the sun again. However small or petty, the distraction can be put to good use when I hold it in the stream of God's light, in a brief act of penitence, thanks, or intercession, or as a request for help. Then I can gently but deliberately let it go.

Giving God our distractions is like handing over a parcel to someone else when we need to have our hands free. In most prayer-times we will end up doing this more than once.

The reason we feel guilty when daydreams come into prayer is that we know we are not giving God our full attention. It is healthy that this should bother us. But most distractions are not sufficiently important for us to become too agitated over them. Absolute, unbroken concentration is very rare.

We don't apply such rigorous standards to ourselves in other spheres, such as an afternoon's hospital visiting. Our main intention then is to be with someone who is ill. We may chat or sit quietly, and probably during the visit our mind will wander off into a few other concerns. But that doesn't take away our basic desire to give our attention to our friend. We won't be plunged into great pangs of guilt if we did think about our journey home or the jobs to be done, while we were at our friend's bedside.

Similarly in prayer, the essential thing is our underlying intention to be with God. If we are doing our best to honour that, the odd distraction doesn't much matter. Instead of becoming tense and irritated when memories and thoughts clatter through our minds, it is better to treat them lightly. A short word or phrase, such as "Abba Father", or "My Lord and my God", or the name "Jesus", can help to draw our attention back into line.

Far more dangerous is the distraction of spiritual pride: "I'm doing rather well at prayer!" That is the biggest distraction of all, and we need to turn our attention quickly away from our own imagined progress and back to God.

Cars and pots

A friend of mine prays regularly in a small chapel, where you can always hear the traffic outside. When this noise becomes a distraction, she uses it as intercession for people travelling, especially one particular member of her church whose job involves a lot of driving. So a sound which could be an annoyance is turned into something positive.

It is said that while St Francis was praying one day, his eye fell on a small pot which he had made. When he realised that his mind had wandered, he picked up the pot and smashed it. If I followed that principle in my living-room, there would be precious little left! Daring to disagree with so great a saint, I think I would prefer to give thanks for the pot, before turning back to God.

I have some rather lopsided but extremely precious clay pots and figures which my children made for me at school. If my eye wanders onto those, the children can be brought into my prayer, in thankfulness and intercession. Then . . . let go!

* * *

When a soul is completely given to Christ . . . there is a complete quieting of self. Only in the willingness to be conformed to God's will can true silence be found.

Stillness of mind leads on to stillness of soul . . . so that the soul may be the true mirror that reflects the light of God.

Mother Mary Clare[19]

O Holy Spirit of God —
come into my heart and fill me:
I open the window of my soul to let Thee in.
I surrender my whole life to Thee:
Come and possess me, fill me with light and truth.

I offer to Thee the one thing I really possess,
My capacity for being filled by Thee.
Of myself I am an empty vessel.
Fill me so that I may live the life of the Spirit,
The life of Truth and Goodness,
The life of Beauty and Love,
The life of Wisdom and Strength.

But, above all, make Christ to be formed in me,
That I may dethrone self in my heart
And make Him King;
So that He is in me, and I in Him,
Today and forever. Amen.[20]

PART 3

Misfortunes, Fears and Frustrations

The choice before the Christian is not whether he shall suffer or whether he shall not, but whether, given suffering, it shall be enlarging and enriching to the Body of Christ, or dwarfing and stunting.

Robert Llewelyn[1]

Blessed are they whose strength is in thee; who going through the vale of misery use it for a well (Psalm 84:5–6, BCP).

Who Shakes a Fist at God

No easy explanations can be given to parents of dying children or to the victims of horrific accidents which maim and kill innocent people.

Christianity is not about rescuing God from blame in the face of disasters; it is a way of living through our hell with him. And that means absolute freedom to let fly at God when we need to, with all our anger, frustration and grief.

Ever since human beings have had the capacity to love and rejoice and laugh, they have also wept and mourned and beaten the ground in despair and anger. The Bible contains several instances of people raging against God over their misfortunes.

"Thou hast made us like sheep for slaughter," complains the Psalm-writer, "the taunt of our neighbours, a laughing-stock among the people. All this has come upon us, though we have not forgotten thee" (from Psalm 44:11–17, RSV).

The great prophet Jeremiah even called God a "deceitful brook" with "waters that fail", at one of his most despairing moments (Jeremiah 15:18).

We too need to be confident enough to pour all our feelings out to God when misfortune strikes. Stiff devotional upper lips are out.

Some people seem to think that the job of religion is to clothe eveything unpleasant in holy language, so that the dead have "gone to a better place", the sick have "joined the band of martyrs", and all misfortunes are "little things sent to try us".

I cringe when such ideas are pushed upon people who are facing unhappiness. I remember at my own mother's funeral, when I was sixteen, how it grated when a lady grabbed my arm and said, "Don't cry, dear; Jesus wanted her."

When people are at their most vulnerable, they do not want to be told what they ought to be thinking. They need to be accepted as they are, and given space. This is how God treats us, and we are not good ambassadors of him if we try to force pious interpretations of events onto people in his name.

It is not that religious insights about suffering are wrong; there *is* an important place for thinking through our pain in the light of God's activity with us and in us. But that comes later, and is the fruit of something else. The first basic need is to be absolutely open and honest with God.

A priest who spends much time counselling the bereaved[2] has seen inner healing take place in many people, when they were able to let go and give vent to their grief and their anger with God. At first they were stunned, and closed to any idea of praying. But when gently encouraged to pour out all the bitterness inside them, they often felt relieved, because the worst had been said. Instead of saying, "I can't pray," their misery had itself become prayer.

Some of these people were surprised to experience a sense of profound peace. One described this as being "wrapped in love . . . in spite of the pain".[3]

If we are politely insincere with God, we build a wall

between us and him. Finding easy "reasons" for suffering may keep him theologically respectable, but we are only protecting the idol of a safe and predictable deity, and losing touch with the true God in the process. You cannot let God off the hook! Don't be afraid to tell him so. He can take it; he always has.

* * *

Dame Cicely Saunders, a pioneer in the Hospice Movement, said on BBC Radio 4 (27th September, 1987):

Both the people who are dying and their friends and relations and lovers must be free to express all their negative feelings and be angry with God if they want to. Often when you've expressed something it loses its power.

And it's often by getting into anger that you find the real cause of many problems that have existed between you and the dying person. Because death is coming, we sometimes see families resolve problems in a short time; you move fast in a crisis. And it's much easier if everyone is being honest.

Who Shakes a Fist At God

Job looks craven:
   Why didn't he fling the crockery?

Elijah under the furze bush fell to depression,
Hungry after running.

Jonah wanted it both ways:
Denunciation of Nineveh,
And the destruction of Nineveh.

Then, as cancer burgeons
Like weed; when the long
Fracture of infidelity stings the heart;
Or we get fired; or somewhere
A child dies against reason,

We'd lie, Lord, on the floor
And shriek; or throw a thick fist
At your love.

Love?
The dreadful sweat
Among old olives came out as
Bravery, elated mercy.
"I have," you affirm, "been already there,
Am acquainted with the hot finger of Providence,
How it feels,
From bruise
Through to blossom."

"I am there now."

John P. White

Through and Beyond Our "No" to God

People are understandably cautious about the idea of giving a "No" to God. It sounds as if we are saying that it is all right to defy and disobey him, or to turn our backs on him when we feel like it.

Obviously that is not what is meant. But if an overwhelmingly negative feeling is all we have, it is better to give that to God than to give him nothing at all. The very act of letting God have our "no" is, paradoxically, a kind of assent, a way of saying, "Here you are. This is me at the moment. You can have me as I am, clogged up with rebellion, misery, panic, the lot! At least I won't hide anything from you."

"NO!" That's how most of us respond to terrible news, in numb and horrified disbelief.

A distraught wife sobs at the head of a mine shaft after a pit disaster; a shy and lonely man learns that his closest friend has only two months to live; a father tries to take in the news that his daughter has been brutally raped. A negative reaction is entirely natural. And that moment when tragic news comes is supremely the time when we should be able to shout out our "No" to God, along with the whole flood of other emotions.

I come back again and again to Jesus's struggle in the Garden of Gethsemane. Even he said "No": "Father, take this cup away from me." Thank goodness the Gospel-writers were honest enough to record this agonised prayer. It would have been so easy to gloss over it as an embarrass-

129

ment, and give the impression that Jesus strode out through the olive-trees to meet the soldiers without batting an eyelid. Jesus's "No" reveals the cost of what he eventually accepted. His solidarity with our misery is no confidence trick.

It is when we recognise and articulate in prayer the "No" which wells up inside us, as Jesus did that night, that we are given the strength to move on into the pain with God.

Acute crises are not the only factors that can make us want to say "No" to God. We may be worn down by too many demands, or drained by a difficult relationship, so that we feel like saying, "I'm sorry, Lord, but I simply can't take this!"

But what happens *after* we have dared to put our "No" into prayer? Everybody's experience of God is different. Some people find themselves in a spiritual limbo for a period, knowing with their brain that God is there, but unable to feel his presence. It takes courage and perseverance to go on praying and reading the Bible in such a situation, but it is worth the struggle. Others feel an immediate sense of release and healing, because God has been with them at their weakest point and they now feel surrounded by his compassion. Others again may find themselves wrestling with God, in a blind and painful struggle to come to terms with what is wounding them, like Jacob, who wrestled with the Lord all night (Genesis 32:22–32).

* * *

I had to cut myself off, live a life of loneliness. When sometimes

I overcame my fears, oh how brutally was I repelled by the redoubled realization of my bad hearing! . . .

O God, Thou lookest down into the depths of my soul, Thou understandest me; Thou knowest that the love of mankind and the urge to do good live within me . . .

Permit me once again to experience a day of pure happiness! For so long now the inner echo of true joy has remained unknown to me. When, oh God, in the temple of nature and mankind, can I ever find it? Never? Oh, no, that would be too cruel to bear.

(Written by the composer Ludwig Van Beethoven (1770–1827), when he was tortured by his deafness.)[4]

From a friend's letter:

. . . The bad news about S.'s illness really threw me for a week or two. I was rebelling and thrashing about, and feeling that if I stopped thinking about her for a minute (and tensing every muscle in my body in the process) I'd be letting her down. It almost felt like the *opposite* of prayer, and very selfish and exhausting . . .

I had previously been trying to work on very simple "stillness exercises" in meditative prayer. Now I found this almost impossible. But I spent some time just working on being still, and slowly bringing S. and each member of the family into the stillness. It felt like the most strenuous task I'd ever attempted, but certainly helped . . .

Falling to the Ground

> *"Falling to the ground" is a powerful image for a certain kind of praying. Some suffering does, metaphorically, knock us over, and there are no devotional formulas that will provide a quick "pick-up-and-shake" to make everything all right.*
>
> *When we have hit rock bottom we cannot fall any further; but we can cry out to God from where we are – and perhaps discover that he is there with us, in the depths.*

An episode from a recent cowboy film sticks in my mind. An angry ranch-owner shouts at one of his cow-hands, "If your daughter thinks she's going to marry my son, she's as good as dead!"

At these words, the girl's father groans and falls to the ground.

"Whatever's the matter with him?" asks the ranch-owner.

A second man replies, "I'm a doctor. I've just had to tell him that his daughter has inoperable cancer. *She is indeed as good as dead.*"

What struck me about this scene was the way it seemed absolutely natural for the father to fall down. People don't usually do this when they are distressed. But it made sense at that moment, as a far more real expression of the man's grief than any angry retort or violent gesture.

As a sixteen-year-old, when my mother was dying, I often threw myself onto the floor and sobbed when I was alone in the house. Looking back, I can see that this expressed a fundamental need. There was a sense of abandonment, as if I was falling with God into the darkness and pain of it all.

"Underneath are the everlasting arms" (Deuteronomy 33:27).

Jesus also fell to the ground. In the Garden of Gethsemane he fell on his face and prayed in anguish to his Father (Matthew 26:39). He must have fallen down, exhausted, while he was carrying the heavy cross-beam through the Jerusalem streets, because we are told that someone else had to bear it for him (Luke 23:26). And to crucify him, they would have pushed him down to lie flat while they drove in the nails. This extraordinary depth of vulnerability is at the heart of God and of the Christian gospel.

"Unless a grain of wheat falls into the earth and dies, it remains alone; but if it dies, it bears much fruit" (John 12:24).

John the Baptist was thrown into the earth, imprisoned in the dungeon beneath Herod Antipas's palace. In a great agony of doubt he began to wonder if everything he had lived and waited for was an illusion. Was Jesus really the messiah after all? In desperation John sent a message to Jesus, "Are you he who is to come, or shall we look for another?" (Matthew 11:3).

Here was the great preacher, falling flat on his face into a hell of uncertainty that must have been far worse than the physical hardship of imprisonment. All he could do was put his questioning into words and offer it to Christ.

We should not be afraid to fall to the ground in prayer, either literally or metaphorically. It is a way of surrendering ourselves into the arms of God when hard things happen to us.

God in the rubble

A terrible disaster overwhelmed the Welsh village of Aberfan in 1966, when a heap of coal slag slid down a mountain and half-buried a street, killing people in many buildings, including children in a school. One teacher died when she threw herself on top of one of her pupils to save his life. Many people said, "Where was God on that day?"

God was there, under the rubble, suffering with those people. And he was especially in that teacher, and all the brave people who risked their lives for the sake of others.

* * *

Out of the depths I cry to thee, O Lord!
  Lord, hear my voice.
I wait for the Lord, my soul waits,
  and in his word I hope (Psalm 130:1, 5).

I am bowed down and brought so low
  that I go mourning all the day long.
I am numbed and stricken to the ground,
  I cry aloud in the yearning of my heart (Psalm 38:6,8)

No matter how low we have fallen, God is beneath us, a

bedrock underlying everything. We can never fall out of his care.

I love thee, O. Lord my strength.
The Lord is my rock, and my fortress, and my deliverer,
    my God, my rock, in whom I take refuge.
In my distress I called upon the Lord,
    to my God I cried for help.

(Psalm 18:1,2,6)

... When we are beaten down and lie flat with our mouths in the dust, hoping for hope ... then we become aware that the whole meaning of our life is a poverty and emptiness, which, far from being a defeat, are really the pledge of all the great supernatural gifts ...

Freedom is found in dependence upon God ... For God's love is like a river springing up in the depth and flowing endlessly through His creation, filling all things with life and goodness and strength.

Thomas Merton[5]

In the Face of Mystery

Many painful things are a mystery, from the cruel accidents of the natural world to the unreasonable ways of the human race. We would feel better if God would shrink himself into our tidy, logical schemes, so that we could explain everything and not feel so much at the mercy of irrational forces. But instead God takes the heart of the mystery of pain into himself.

One tempting "solution" to the existence of suffering is to say that God deliberately inflicts it on us because it is good for us. Heaven forbid. The life and work of Jesus make it abundantly clear that God works for the healing of disease and the alleviation of human misery. The way a cut finger heals up is an instance of the recuperative force which works in our bodies most of the time. When Christ heals, he harnesses and magnifies that same, God-given energy.

In Swaziland, where we lived for some years, babies often died of diarrhoea because of dirty feeding-bottles and rampant viruses. Parents would sometimes say, "It is God's will." But I could not accept that. There is a difference between what God wills directly, and what he allows to happen because the world is what it is. You can see this distinction on a domestic level. When parents allow their teenage son to go on a bicycle-ride, their permission includes the risk of his being knocked down and killed. But they do not directly will that outcome, and are filled with grief it it happens.

So with God. His creation is a huge risk, and the delicate balance of conditions necessary for life to exist at all can go crazily wrong. We have bodies which feel pain, water which drowns as well as saves, fire which warms as well as wounds, and rock which supports us but can break apart in earthquakes. Yet God does not deliberately engineer human misery.

The fact that we ask why famines happen and babies die is evidence for hope. God could have made us heartless automatons; instead we are on the side of life and love – and that hurts.

God is always beyond us. We cannot summon him like

a genie from a lamp, to give every story a happy ending, or provide a rational explanation for all bad situations. Suffering remains a mystery. What God has done, however, is to take into himself the consequences of his world, on the Cross.

Our response to suffering can only be a mixture of anger and wonder. Faced with the irrational elements of human life, it is perhaps better during prayer not to try and work out reasons, but to remain silent in the darkness with God.

Death itself is a mystery. When someone dies we ask, "Where *is* he, where *is* she?" However deep our faith that life goes on, we still find it hard to accept the fact that a person we love is not around any more.

"You'll get over it," people say. Bereavement is so easy to dismiss in the unwitting cruelty of kindly platitudes. But you do not "get over it", in the way that you get over the flu or a disappointing interview.

Time, in my experience, does not heal the sense of loss, even if it heals the grief. Over the years, praying about the people we have lost becomes a mixture of good memories, painful longings – and silence.

* * *

In the presence of mystery, what we must do is let the mystery be. Allow the mystery the fullness of its own being . . . allow God to be God.

John Main[6]

137

No Certainty, No Control

One of the disconcerting things about misfortune is that familiar and comfortable elements of life are stripped away, and events move out of our control. This is a wilderness experience and it can be frightening. Yet God is there, in the chilly emptiness, even though we may not be aware of him at the time.

Accident or illness can deprive you of ordinary, homely things, like going for a walk with your family or friends, or sitting down to a Christmas dinner together. Security is being taken away from you, you worry because the future for you and your family is so uncertain, and a sense of loneliness creeps in.

Words like "Cheer up, you're in the wilderness with Jesus!" are no help at all. You just want to get away from such a bleak landscape, and it is right to share with God all your misery and anxiety.

But in the end, there is nothing for it but to accept the fact that this is your particular wilderness at present. It seems harsh to put it like that. Yet this is where you are, and this is where God is with you, not half-way down the road on some imaginary escape route, but here.

None of us likes having control taken away from us. As parents we long to be able to *do* something when our children are unhappy or insecure; but sometimes there is absolutely nothing we can do, other than suffer with them. For ourselves, too, there are moments when we wish we could press a magic button to put things right. But Christian faith is not about controlling events with the help of God (although some people appear to see prayer in this way). Prayer is the opposite of control – it is letting go of our lives and wills into God's life and will.

The very fact of being a Christian means that we live by faith and not proof (Hebrews 11:1); accepting a degree of uncertainty is part of our vocation. When Jesus sent his followers out in pairs to preach the gospel, he would not let them take any emergency supplies (Luke 10:3–4); managing without security was somehow essential to their task.

When trouble hits us, we may find we can no longer rely on what we can do ourselves, so we are thrown back onto God. It is then that he invites us to step out with him into the unknown.

In her book *Beyond all Pain*[7], Dame Cicely Saunders describes the struggle of Enid at St Christopher's Hospice:

> Enid fought her way to peace, and we often had to battle alongside her. She found her profound dependence hard to bear, and could be difficult and demanding. Such struggles towards acceptance are often prolonged, as the same battle is fought over and over again . . . She asked sometimes angry but honest questions of the God she deeply believed in and had served during her active life, and after a long battle she gradually accepted the reality of what was happening, and found the answer, which she has left us, dictated during the month before she died:
>
> > A friend and I were considering life and its purpose. I said, even with increasing paralysis and loss of

speech, I believed there is a purpose for my life, but I was not sure what it was. We agreed to pray about it ... I was then sure that my present purpose is simply to receive other people's prayers and kindness, and to link together all those who are lovingly concerned about me. My friend said, "It must be hard to be the wounded Jew, when, by nature, you would rather be the Good Samaritan." It is hard. It would be unbearable, were it not for my belief that the wounded man and the Samaritan are inseparable. It was the helplessness of the one that brought out the best in the other and linked them together.

* * *

The Lord found his people in a desert land,
    and in the howling waste of the wilderness;
He encircled them, he cared for them,
    He kept them as the apple of his eye.
Like an eagle that stirs up its nest,
    that flutters over its young,
Spreading out its wings, catching them,
    bearing them on its pinions (Deuteronomy 32:10–11).

            I know
that when the stress has grown too strong,
        Thou wilt be there.
            I know
that when the waiting seems so long,
        Thou hearest prayer.
            I know
that through the crash of falling worlds,

Thou holdest me.
    I know
that life and death are Thine
    Eternally.

The Rev Mother Stuart[8]

Lord, even when I cannot find you, you are still there.

Things Going Wrong

When we are doing what we believe to be God's will, we generally expect him to do his bit and look after our project. If things start going wrong we get very steamed up, and our confidence can be badly shaken.

Yet part of our job as Christians is to taste what it is like not to be in a position of strength, especially if we are concerned to help the underprivileged. We find ourselves side by side with them – and closer to Christ – when we are vulnerable ourselves.

We easily forget that things sometimes went wrong for Jesus. When he came down from the stunning mountain-top experience of the transfiguration, he found his disciples struggling in vain to heal an epileptic boy (Mark 9:14–29). Even when he had just performed his sublime action with bread and wine at the Last Supper, the disciples began bickering about which among them was the greatest (Luke 22:24). That must be the most poignant anti-climax in history.

141

Absolute power can be demonic, as Jesus knew when he was shaken by temptations in the wilderness. "Why don't you take the easy way?" whispered the devil. "Get popular quickly, impress everyone with a 'Superman' trick and jump off the Temple pinnacle. Coerce people into loving you, and avoid all the misunderstanding and pain. You can do it! Just worship me; do things my way, and you'll have the whole world at your feet!" (from Matthew 4:1–11).

But Jesus said "No", choosing instead a way of limitation and suffering; and he is still with us in the misery of our weakness and uncertainty. The very fact of the Incarnation, God becoming man, reveals God's own mysterious vulnerability and self-emptying. It is not his way to provide us with a safety-rail; instead he invites us to walk on the water with him.

* * *

For the sake of Christ, then, I am content with weaknesses, insults, hardships, persecutions, and calamities; for when I am weak, then I am strong. (2 Cor. 12:10).

Praying with Failure

Failure is a wilderness all of its own, an arid and comfortless ache of disappointment, humiliation and frustration.
   Rational arguments do not help much: "We can't all shine. Everyone has strengths and weaknesses. You wouldn't

want to succeed under false pretences, would you?" *Our heart is still as heavy as lead. We have, in a sense, been stripped by the experience, and stand helpless before God.*

Thomas Merton once wrote, "The desert is the logical dwelling place for the man who seeks to be . . . solitary and poor, and dependent upon no one but God."[9] The miserable experience of failure brings us into such a desert whether we like it or not. For that reason it is supremely a time when we can honestly say, "Lord, I am nothing; you are all."

Many people – and notoriously Christians – impose upon themselves and others a crippling anxiety about "getting things right". Individuals struggle to live up to the straight-jacket of a so-called "ideal Christian life"; clergy are ground down by what appears from the outside to be failure and division in the parish, and church congregations experience loss of confidence if numbers fall.

But the way of Jesus is not one of success in worldly terms. His disciples constantly got their doctrine wrong, and let him down into the bargain. They misunderstood him (Mark 8:17), lacked faith (Mark 9:19), and abandoned him at the end (Mark 14:50). Yet their commitment during Jesus's earthly ministry and in the early church was crucial. It would have been a tragic loss if these men had refused to follow Jesus because they were nervous about making mistakes.

Of course we should try to be as generous and loving and true to Christ as we can. And of course we want the best possible outcome in our work for the kingdom of God. But the results of our efforts are God's, not ours. Christ liberates us from the need to rely on ourselves alone, and from the fear of failure, which can be such a heavy burden. As has often been said, God does not ask us for success, only for faithfulness. And when we offer our mistakes to God he sometimes uses them in ways that take us by surprise.

The congregation were unanimous that it was the best sermon the vicar had ever preached. He was a shy bachelor, extremely clever, and not always easy to understand. But this week everyone had listened. It was a baptism, and he had told them how he used to be terrified of small children, and dreaded visiting his younger brother, who had twins. He described how he used to trip over their toys because he was short-sighted, and wondered what to talk to the children about, and what to give them for presents.

One day his brother and sister-in-law had gone out unexpectedly while he was there, leaving him as baby-sitter. He did his best to play with the children and read to them, but he panicked when one of them spilt paint on the carpet. Then they started to argue and hit each other. To his embarrassment the twins were both screaming at the top of their voices when Mum and Dad came back! He felt a complete failure – even though afterwards his brother told him that the children liked it when he came because he was so "peaceful"!

The vicar went on to say how he sometimes visited homes where parents felt inadequate. "God has given you a task which is never easy, and you can't avoid mistakes, as I discovered in my brief baby-sitting days. Children make you vulnerable," he said, "but they also make you alive."

* * *

If any one among you thinks that he is wise in this age, let him become a fool, that he may become wise. For the wisdom of this world is folly with God.

For all things are yours; and you are Christ's, and Christ is God's (1 Corinthians 3:18–23).

The human heart longs for a true bonding, a true communion, which doesn't say, "I'll love you if you are successful or clever or attractive." We all yearn to be told, "I love you because you ARE."

This is pure love, the real thing, like pure gold or pure water. And Christ loves us with that incredible, unconditional love.

Jean Vanier[10]

FEAR, ANXIETY AND DOUBT

The Shapes of Fear

Fear takes many forms. Sometimes it is a permanent and uncomfortable part of our landscape. At other times it is so acute that it threatens to overwhelm us.

Praying through our fear does not take it away. But by looking it in the eye and naming it before God, we are more likely to find the strength to hold it rather than be held by it.

What do you fear? Illness? Nuclear war? Loneliness? Most of us struggle with fears and worries at some point in our lives. Fear is natural, but we need to find ways of facing and harnessing it, rather than letting it dominate us.

Four primary shapes of fear could be identified as: the knife, the tight necklace, the cloud, and the coward. There is also "positive fear", which is rather different.

The knife

This is the most agonising of all types of fear, a cruel thrust of dread in the midriff, when it seems that something terrible is happening: your child may die, your husband may be lost on a mountaineering expedition, you yourself may have inoperable cancer . . .

The tight necklace

This is almost as bad, the choking panic that comes if you think you are about to be mugged, or your car is going to crash, or the building you are in is on fire. Lesser forms of this fear crop up at other alarming moments: when people hear a noise in the house and think it's a burglar, or when they suddenly panic in a lonely place.

The cloud

We imagine all sorts of horrific things happening to our children and grandchildren. We are afraid of losing our friends, or of not being able to pay the bills. Such dark and chilly clouds cling heavily, almost physically at times.

The coward

This is a niggling anxiety, such as fear of unpopularity, fear of the dentist, or fear of facing up to a demand that we know we should meet.

Positive fear

In contrast to the other types, which all have a miserable aspect, this is a good fear, springing from concern and compassion. You see positive fear when people are involved in the welfare of others, and are anxious on their behalf.

It is also a positive fear when we are afraid of letting God down or of betraying our own consciences.

Other people will identify different shapes. Whatever they may be, it is useful to sort out our fears, as part of the process of recognising and praying through them.

* * *

Lord, I am frightened.

I am trying to pray, but my anxiety keeps coming to mind and taking over. Let my fear become my prayer, as I try to recognise it and give it to you. Deepen my trust, and help me to abandon myself into your hands.

The Knife – Fear that Overwhelms

Some fear is so overpowering that we cannot hold or handle it ourselves. All we can do is stay still with God, in the middle of it. Even doing that is a way of facing the fear, however helpless we feel.

Intense fear can drive us along, like a tyrant with a whip. I remember the sensation of being driven by panic as I walked blindly through hospital corridors, when our three-month-old son was about to undergo heart surgery. I went out into the street and resented the fact that everyone around me was happily carrying on a normal existence while my child was fighting for his life. The monster fear held me in an iron jaw.

"I hate having to say this to parents, but I cannot promise that your baby is going to pull through." During the three terrible days after the hospital consultant had said that to us, the only prayer that made any sense was simply, "Oh God, don't let him die, please . . ."

For many hours the sense of fear almost paralysed me, and I could only stand before God, numb and wretched. But there was one extraordinary moment when I sensed the power of love that was holding Andrew. I described this in an earlier book:

> One morning while sitting with Andrew, whose body was a mass of tubes and wires linked to machines, I suddenly knew that he was in God's hands, what-ever should happen. I realised that he was loved and held by God, whether he recovered from this illness or not . . . This moment of heightened awareness lasted for only a short time. I soon became distraught again . . .[11]

While Andrew's condition was critical, I both trusted God and didn't trust him, at the same time. Fear was never far away until the consultant was at last able to say to us, "He's got a good chance now."

I learned that praying with fear is a matter of hanging on to what we believe deep down, even when we cannot feel it to be true at the time. We have somehow to keep hold of God's promise to be with us, reaching out to him even when everything is grim and empty. "Trusting fear" or "fear-filled trust" sound a contradiction in terms. But that is the way God's grace works in us when we are facing the acute stab of the knife of fear.

* * *

My God, my God, why have you forsaken me?
   why are you so far from helping me
   and from the words of my groaning?
I am poured out like water
   and all my bones are out of joint:
   my heart within me is like melting wax.
O Lord, do not stand far off:
   You are my helper, hasten to my aid.

                     (Psalm 22:1, 14, 19)

O God, You know we are often filled with fear and
  foreboding.
Give us courage, and deepen our trust.
You are a rock which nothing can shatter.
On You we place the whole weight of our lives.

                     Richard Harries[12]

The Tight Necklace – Should We Feel Afraid?

Sometimes people think that "real Christians" should never feel afraid, and that fear betrays a weakness of faith.

    You do hear of outstanding individuals who go unconcerned into dangerous situations, knowing that Jesus is with them. But

*such courage is rare, and most of us do fear things like violence,
illness and insecurity. Trust would not be trust if we were not
sometimes afraid.*

'Tight-necklace" fear, which we feel when something terrible might happen, is a perfectly natural reaction, and the
obvious prayer is simply, "Help!"

My children and I once went on a pleasure-trip in a
small fishing-boat round some islands off the south coast
of Wales. It was a blustery day, and as we went further
out into the open sea, the boat was thrown around alarm-
ingly, and the waves roared and surged from a great height
all round us. All the passengers looked very frightened. I
remember, in the constricting sensation of fear, trying to
reassure the children, and praying continually under my
breath, "Lord, help us." Most of us do that in a crisis.

But not all our fears are so acute.

Take my fear of pain at the dentist. This superficial fear
is overridden by a more sensible anxiety, that my teeth
might fall out if I did not have the necessary fillings. And
greater than both those fears is my trust that the dentist
knows what he is doing. That confidence in my dentist's
skill is what makes my fears bearable and gives me the
courage (albeit wobbly) to face the treatment.

Although this cannot be pushed too far as a religious
allegory, it is a useful image of the way our fears vary in
depth and value, and how they can all be put into a wider
context of trust in God.

Suppose someone finds himself required to make an
unpopular stand for what he believes to be right. If he is
afraid of being scorned by the others, that is "coward

fear". But he may also be afraid of betraying the truth as he sees it, and fear the loss of his own integrity. When any of us faces a similar situation, we have to pray that God will enable our good or "positive" fears to overrule the others.

* * *

Russian Orthodox Christian, Mikhail Kukobaka, has spent five years in Soviet psychiatric hospitals and eleven years in prisons and labour camps, because of his defence of freedom of speech. At the time of writing, he is still in a strict régime camp, though great efforts are being made for his release[13]. In an open letter to the Soviet Minister of Health in 1979, which led to his re-arrest, he wrote:

> *I am frightened of prison, of camps, of lunatic asylums ... but I am more frightened of lies, base behaviour, and my own participation in either of these, than of any prison. I am not ashamed to be called a prisoner ... I want to live according to my convictions.*

The Cloud – What About the Future?

> *One aspect of fear which can grow out of all proportion is anxiety about the future. But much of this is pure speculation, things which might never happen. We are only given grace to cope with the present moment; nobody can carry the burdens of next month and next year as well.*

We picture all sorts of terrible things happening in the future which may never arise: What if all our plans go wrong? How would we cope in such and such a crisis? What if . . .?

The world can seem a dangerous place into which to bring our children. We would not be human if we didn't worry at times. Yet, if we let go of undue worry about the future and concentrate on what God wants of us here and now, unexpected things can happen to enhance the quality of life in the present.

Numerous Christians can testify to this. Having committed themselves to giving generously of their time and resources in serving Christ, many people have found help and opportunities coming unexpectedly; there have been testing moments, but God has not deserted them. They have discovered what Jesus meant by "seeking first the kingdom of God", and entrusting everything else to him.

Do not be anxious about your life, what you shall eat or what you shall drink, nor about your body, what you shall put on. Is not life more than food, and the body more than clothing?

Seek first the kingdom of God, and his righteousness, and all these things shall be yours as well (Matthew 6:25, 33).

We can never strike a bargain with God or tempt him ("I'll do your will, so you look after me"). But giving our attention to what he wants in the present moment puts worry about the future into a different perspective.

This is not to say that we should avoid saving, or planning ahead, or taking out life insurance. Such things help us to deal with future needs and then forget about them. But the significant question remains: is anxiety about the future so dominating our lives that we can spare little thought for what God is asking of us now?

> *If one day I should go out of my mind,*
> *Lord, let me still be Yours, even if I cease*
> *to understand what being "Yours" may mean.*
> *I fear mental illness, change of nature,*
> *the indignity of people saying, "Poor soul,*
> *she's not the person that she used to be."*
> *Lord, if I go insane,*
> *let my condition be*
> *an offering for the millions*
> *of others who have faced*
> *inner confusion and the loss of self.*
> *O God, even my fear of "going mad"*
> *is outstripped by Your love*
> *into eternity.*
>
> *So help me to forget about tomorrow,*
> *and concentrate on living in today.*

If we live, we live to the Lord, and if we die, we die to the Lord; so then, whether we live or whether we die, we are the Lord's (Romans 14:8).

The Coward – Fear of Other People

The herd instinct is often too strong for us. We want to belong and be like everybody else, and we dread the moment when eyebrows are raised and glances exchanged over something we have said or done.

Sometimes people try to threaten or bully us into conforming. It takes courage not to live up to other people's expectations; it takes prayer to live up to God's – and be ourselves.

I once knew a young white South African couple (I'll call them Phil and Jane) who lived in Johannesburg. They made friends with several black people from work and from the Cathedral congregation where they worshipped. Black colleagues often came to have supper with them.

Because of this, insulting letters began to come through the letter-box from other tenants in their block of flats (who were all white – by law), with insinuations that they might be forced to leave. Jane and Phil resisted this and went on as before, though by now their immediate neighbours openly snubbed them.

Phil and Jane are profoundly prayerful people. Their freedom springs from being soaked in something greater than the desire to be liked and accepted. They often stay with a community of contemplative nuns in Lesotho, finding that the atmosphere of contemplative prayer there helps to purify their desire to obey God.

Phil and Jane are honest about their fear of harassment; but they also have something deeper on which to draw.

This reminds me of the courage of Peter and John in the Acts of the Apostles, when they were hauled before the Jewish authorities. The high priest reprimanded them for teaching people about Jesus, and told them not to do it again. With the glorious serenity of a person who is totally given to Christ, Peter replied, "We must obey God rather than men" (Acts 5:27–42).

A common factor in all these brave people is that they are absorbed in the God who is, for them, stronger and greater than the things they fear. Their prayerful dependence on God gives them the courage and the freedom to discover their true selves.

Praying with the fear of conflict

Ponder for a moment: do I help others by pretending to agree with them, or letting them rule my life?

Take the clashes between Jesus and the Pharisees. Suppose he had changed his mind, and agreed not to heal on the Sabbath, so as not to offend the authorities. Would it have helped anyone?

* * *

Lord, by your grace give me truthfulness, courage and simplicity. Free me from the usual evasions which stop me being myself and let me dare to receive the freedom you hold out to me.

Fear not, little flock, it is my Father's pleasure to give you the kingdom (Luke 12:32).

I am with you always, to the end of time (Matthew 28:20).

Don't fear those who can kill the body, but those who can kill the soul (Luke 12:4).

St Paul writes, "Am I now seeking the favour of men, or of God? If I were still pleasing men, I should not be a servant of Christ" (Galatians 1:10)

Fear in a Wider Framework

Fear is not something to feel guilty about; it is something to put side by side with the infinitely greater power of God's love.

Some time ago I felt frightened when walking alone through a part of London. Houses were shabby, everywhere was run down, and many young people were sitting on the walls outside their houses in twos and threes, sometimes not even talking, but just looking. Increasingly uneasy, I quickened my pace, feeling that their eyes were on me and that I was somehow part of the system that aggravated the hopelessness and depression of those unemployed people.

I came to a Roman Catholic church, and as I had half an hour to spare before a meeting I decided to go in. No sooner had I sat down than some noisy teenagers followed me in and began to make jokes at the back. Then a wayfarer smelling strongly of alcohol came and sat near me.

I wished I could escape to somewhere cosy and safe, where I could feel I "belonged" . . .

Then my eyes fell onto the central figure of Christ on the cross. And I found myself saying, "Lord, if I run away from all this, I am running away from you. You are here, in the middle of all this poverty and purposelessness – and laughter."

I gradually began to accept both my own reactions and the things around me. By saying "yes" to everything there, I was somehow saying "yes" to Christ. I realised that the wayfarer and the teenagers at the back were not a threat, but fellow human beings, created and loved by God.

This was not an earth-shattering experience, nor was I suddenly free from all my nerves. But it was a glimpse, in spite of my thudding heart, of the fact that Christ offers us something greater than our fear. It also taught me how loneliness can be turned into solitude when we are no longer so frightened.

There is a verse in the first Epistle of John, which can make people feel guilty about being afraid: "There is no fear in love, but perfect love casts out fear . . . and he who fears is not perfected in love" (1 John 4:18).

We think to ourselves, "But I do fear certain things, so it must be my fault, and I must be lacking in love."

That is a misunderstanding. The verse needs to be seen in the context of the preceding passage, which is about God's love for us (4:10). It is the "day of judgment" that we need not fear (v 17), because God's love for us is so great. As long as God's love lives in us we have nothing to fear of his punishment (v 18). Hence, "perfect love casts out fear".

It is true that the more we love God, the less we are ruled by fears for ourselves. On a human level too, the more secure we feel in the love of other people, the less we fear a disagreement with them. But this is quite different from saying that it is sinful or unloving to be afraid.

The agony which made Jesus sweat blood in the Garden of Gethsemane must surely have included human fear. And Jesus lacked neither trust nor love. For him, as for us, certain things are indeed fearful. Yet for him, as for us, there is something stronger and deeper: the steady love of God, who sustains us through and beyond all our vulnerability.

* * *

A monk of the Egyptian Coptic Church described how he used to be afraid of wolves, when he was in his lonely desert hermitage. But then he realised that they, too, were creatures made by God.
They did him no harm.

May I be without fear,
   by night and by day.
Let all the world be my friend.[14]

Positive Fear – The Other Side of Hope

The fact that we fear many things is not totally negative. We only feel afraid because we have a basic sense that life is valuable, with a purpose and meaning that we want to protect. Like guilt, fear makes a useful servant but a bad master.

Praying with our worries is a sifting and sorting process, because God enables us to see which things really matter, and which we need to let go of.

Fear can be useful when it stops us doing dangerous and foolish things. If a small child is completely fearless we all start agitating: he might touch the fire, run into the road, or walk straight off a cliff.

Some of our anxiety for other people, or for issues which really matter, is "positive fear", and could be said to be the price of loving. Other fears are a form of selfishness which need to go into the dustbin. Maybe we are pinning too much hope on our job, reputation or standard of living, and need to loosen our worried grip on these things. Perhaps our concern as parents is in danger of becoming over-protectiveness. Praying with God about all our uneasiness helps us to distinguish between the sensible and the not-so-sensible kinds of fear.

Some people are worriers by nature and need to let go of excessive misgivings; others are more happy-go-lucky, and should perhaps feel more anxiety, not less, about the things that threaten our human community. God is not going to change any of us into different people; but he can bring out our hidden capacity to rise above our weaknesses, so that we become "caring happy-go-lucky" people, or "brave worriers". Prayer is where our limitation meets God's greatness.

Many of our fears are the cost of living in a marvellous yet dangerous world. To possess something precious is to risk losing it; sharing this planet with other people means that we might be hurt by them. We are never totally secure, but few of us would want to live in a perfectly safe and insulated box.

God's love is stronger than all our evil. We, the human race, did our worst at the crucifixion, and attempted to kill God in Jesus. Yet he rose from the dead, and is with us in a more far-reaching way than ever before. Absolutely nothing can beat him now, and he gives us a bedrock of hope beneath even the worst of our fears.

Even the horrific prospect of a nuclear holocaust – a trauma so deadly that we can hardly imagine it – is contained within Calvary. The cross was God's own holocaust, the place where he was wholly burned out for us, and from it came the triumphant cry: "It is accomplished! It is finished!" (John 19:30) – "We've won!"

Many worries and fears are like the clouds that cover parts of the earth, on those magnificent photographs of our planet taken from the moon. Looked at from a distance, we see that they are only part of something far greater than themselves.

* * *

Fear not, says the Lord, for I have redeemed you,
I have called you by name, you are mine.

When you pass through the waters I will be with you,
  and through the rivers, they shall not overwhelm you;
When you walk through fire you shall not be burned,
  and the flame shall not consume you.
For I am the Lord your God,
  the Holy One of Israel, your Saviour (Isaiah 43:1b–3).

Doubt

Faith would not be faith without an element of doubt, any more than courage would be courage if we did not feel afraid. Praying with doubt is part of our searching and longing for God.

None of us can ever grasp everything there is to know about God. It is absurd to demand absolute certainty from anyone. On the contrary, it is those who have prayed and loved God most who have always had the strongest sense that he is unfathomable.

If we reckon we have a totally comprehensible God, we are in danger of idolatry, because we think we can contain him within our own definitions. That is to reduce him to a "thing" that can be held in our finite minds. Yet God is essentially infinite and beyond us, so that religious experience must include an element of not-knowing. As St Paul says, "Now we see in a mirror, dimly." "How unsearchable are his judgments and how inscrutable his ways!" (1 Corinthians 13:12; Romans 11:33).

Living and praying as Christians sometimes means persevering with a mixture of faith and doubt, which can be very painful. We long for some final proof, to put an end to the uncomfortable challenge to our beliefs. Surprisingly, things which seemed a threat to our faith at one time can become a help later, in our search for a deeper understanding of God and his ways. The main thing is that we are open with him about our doubts, even when it is his very existence that we are questioning.

* * *

Lord, even You know what it is like to feel as if "God is no more", to wonder if what you've staked your whole life on is after all just an illusion. You know what it is like to keep going in the dark by a sheer act of will; to go on loving when there seems to be no response; to abandon oneself to a divine providence one can neither see nor feel. Lord, when it is dark and we cannot feel your presence, and nothing seems real any more, and we are tempted to give up trying – help us to know that you are never really absent – that we are like a little child in its mother's arms, held so close to your heart that we cannot see your face; and that underneath are the everlasting arms.

Margaret Dewey[15]

ILLNESS

Praying in Illness

When we are ill, we generally don't feel like praying very much. Instead of trying to stick to our normal ways of spending time with God, it is a relief to discover another way of praying – a more passive kind, a letting go into God. It doesn't matter if we do not have much drive or energy of our own, because prayer is as much God's activity as ours.

What sort of a God do we think he is?

If we are ill, nobody expects us to leap onto a train and go to work, or dash round the house spring-cleaning. Most people understand that we cannot function normally, so surely God does!

He knows how unwell we are feeling. He is not going to force us into demanding systems of prayer, like some harsh Dickensian headmaster. Illness is supremely the time when we should "pray as we can, and not as we can't".[16]

A sick and weary body can say certain things that cannot be conveyed quite so deeply when we are hale and hearty. We are used to the idea that the body expresses praise or devotion in ordinary worship, by kneeling, standing, or sitting with palms of the hands open. In the same way, the very act of lying down when we are ill can be a statement of trust and self-abandonment to God. Because we are physically weak we can only surrender ourselves into the Power, greater than ourselves, who is God.

Illness is an opportunity to discover something about the more passive side of praying. Our task is not so much to do things, as to be willing to let God do work in us. This is true of all prayer, and is the paradox which made St Paul say, "When I am weak, then I am strong" (2 Corinthians 12:10).

There is no single way of praying in illness. Some people find prayers of relaxation helpful. But a friend who is constantly facing pain says that such suggestions make her want to scream. For her, trying to relax the body only brings the pain and discomfort into sharper focus, making it even more of an unbearable distraction to prayer.

All we can do is see which of the many possibilities is best for us.

By far the most important thing is the fact that we want to pray at all when we are ill. Our desire for God, however feeble and befuddled, is the heart of the matter, and the way in which our praying works out in practice is secondary. For some people, the knowledge that they want to reach out to God is literally all they can manage. Then they need the prayers of others to help them to express that need for God and take it further (a theme explored in the next section). Single words such as "Lord", "Jesus", or "Abba Father" give us something to repeat and hang on to when nothing else is possible.

Relaxing in prayer

The prayer of relaxation can be particularly useful to those who are exhausted or convalescing, or who have a debilitating ache rather than acute pain to deal with.

Lie still, as relaxed as you can. Put yourself into God's

hands. Starting with the top of your head, concentrate on letting go the muscles all the way through your body, progressing slowly downwards: eyes, back of the throat, neck, shoulders, arms, etc. As you do this, imagine that each part of you is melting, like ice in hot water. Let this melting become your self-abandonment into the warmth and healing power of God, whose love is flowing through you.

A simple prayer to use as you come to each part of your body is: "Jesus – my weakness into your strength."

Holding or touching

Others may prefer to find ways of distracting the body by actually doing something. One possibility is to trace certain shapes with the finger.

David Adam's book, *The Edge of Glory*[17], contains many "encircling" prayers and motifs in the Celtic tradition, which convey how we are surrounded by the divine love.

You could trace with a finger the shapes that accompany these prayers, before, after, or at the same time as using the words themselves:

> The Trinity
> Protecting me
> The Father be
> Over me,
> The Saviour be
> Under me.

The Spirit be
About me,
The Holy Three
Defending me.
As evening come
Bless my home,
Holy Three
Watching me.
As shadows fall
Hear my call.
Sacred Three
Encircle me.
So it may be
Amen to Thee.
Holy Three
About me.

The circle and the triangle remind us of the mystery that God's love is infinite and eternal, without beginning or end.

This Celtic trefoil is another motif which can be traced with a finger, using a prayer such as: "*My Lord, My Love, My Life . . .*" Simply looking at this figure, and thinking the words, might also be a help in focusing your attention away from bodily discomfort and onto God.

Another well known way of doing something while praying is to use the beads of a rosary, while saying a short prayer of love or dependence on God. (I explore this further in the section, *Insomnia and a Rosary*.) Phrases such as "Father, hold me", "Jesus, heal me", "Spirit help me" bear much repeating, and go well with a rhythmic handling of the beads.

There are many variations on that theme: "Father, Jesus, Spirit; hold me, heal me, help me"; or "Hold me, Lord; heal me, Lord; help me, Lord".

Remembering that God is love, and that he enfolds us in his love, single words are often sufficient, such as "God . . . Love . . . God . . .", reciting one word with each bead.

Some people are alarmed at the thought of using a rosary. Obviously there are dangers in this, as in any form of praying. The words could become "vain repetitions"; but this does not have to be so. The beads *could* be regarded as earning points of merit for us in heaven, but this mistaken view could equally be applied to all other forms of meditation and worship. The beads are an aid to prayer, something external to hang on to with our hands, because we want to hang on to God with our hearts.

Knots in a piece of wool can also be used in this way. I know someone who uses her fingers in prayer, one by one, instead of a rosary. There is nothing to stop a sick person holding or just pressing each finger in turn and using short prayers while doing so.

Using psalms

Old favourites like Psalm 23 take a lot of beating when we feel unwell:

The Lord is my shepherd:
therefore can I lack nothing.
He will make me lie down in green pastures:
and lead me beside still waters.
He will refresh my soul,
and guide me in right pathways for his name's sake.
Though I walk through the valley of the shadow of death,
I will fear no evil;
For you are with me,
Your rod and your staff comfort me.

There are other helpful psalms in the ancient night-time office of Compline, for example:

In Thee, O Lord, have I put my trust,
let me never be put to confusion,
deliver me in thy righteousness;
Bow down Thine ear to me,
make haste to deliver me;
And be Thou my strong rock and house of defence,
that Thou mayest save me . . .
. . . Into Thy hands I commend my spirit,
for Thou hast redeemed me, O Lord, Thou God of truth
(Psalm 31:1–5, BCP)

Using the imagination

Some people find the imagination a useful tool in prayer.

Picture Jesus healing people, and then see him walking towards you, looking at you with deep compassion, and stretching out to lay his hands on you.

You could imagine that Jesus takes both your hands in his. Feel the warmth; the love; the sense of security, come what may.

There is another Celtic encircling prayer which you could say as you imagine this:

I place my hands in Yours, Lord,
I place my hands in Yours.

I place my will in Yours, Lord,
I place my will in Yours.

I place my days in Yours, Lord,
I place my days in Yours.

I place my thoughts in Yours, Lord,
I place my thoughts in Yours.

I place my heart in Yours, Lord,
I place my heart in Yours.

I place my hands in Yours, Lord,
I place my hands in Yours.

The Prayers of Others

A hospital chaplain tells me that people often ask him to pray because they feel too ill to do so themselves. Either individually or in a group, this is an important way of helping sick people to be held in the love of God.

Furthermore, being ill can land you with a ministry to all the people round you who want to help.

If you are ill, and friends in the room are praying for you, your part is simply to let go into the hands of God, like lying in a safety-net which is being held by other people. Let them say for you what you cannot say yourself, knowing that you are surrounded and soaked in God's love. Just by being there and consenting for this to happen, you are part of the praying.

The most important thing to realise is that you are accepted and profoundly loved by God, however unsatisfactory or difficult your life. In that fact alone lies the heart of healing.

Christians involved in full-time ministries of prayer for healing usually say that many people are physically healed, but not all. We do not understand why. But what we do know is that God always blesses people through prayer, sometimes in unexpected ways.

Whatever happens to you, the essential truth, which nobody can take away from you, is that *God loves you*. Coming to realise that fact more deeply may itself be a step towards physical recovery.

This is a prayer for a friend to say for you:

The weaving of peace be thine
Peace around thy soul entwine
Peace of the Father flowing free
Peace of the Son sitting over thee
Peace of the Spirit for thee and me
Peace of the One
Peace of the Three
A weaving of peace be upon thee . . .
. . . Around thee twine the Three
The encircling of the Trinity.[18]

Sometimes for a friend just to be present with a sick person is the best way to help, sharing a mutual powerlessness and silence with God.

Being prayed for by other Christians when you are ill may, however, be a mixed blessing. On the one hand, the sensitive and faithful prayer of friends can be an invaluable help. But some people may unwittingly be pressurising you, so that you feel as if you are almost letting the side down if you don't get better. I know a sick person who is surrounded by so many Christians full of zeal for God's power to heal, that they never give him space to say, "I feel dreadful", or a chance to pray through that feeling.

This is intercession gone wrong. Of course we should ask God for healing, and open up to receive whatever he will give us. But it is wrong to feel that physical healing depends on how much teeth-gritting "faith" we can muster. That is a distortion of Christ's healing work, and only adds a burden of guilt to the misery sick people already feel. True faith is having the guts to come to God empty-handed, and to depend totally on him. It is not some feat of will-power, convincing ourselves that we will get what we want out of God, come what may. Healing depends on the will and grace of Christ, not on us.

Another approach is to adopt a lightness of touch in our own mind, and quietly to share the joke with God. So the next time an over-zealous friend insists on laying hands heavily on you and saying, with ever-increasing intensity, "O Lord, forgive this thy child for his lack of faith, and let him claim the total recovery you are definitely offering him, NOW!", will you be able to see the funny side of it? Is it possible to send up your hurt and irritation on an imaginary air balloon, and to ask for blessing and the gentle touch of God's Holy Spirit, both for the person praying and for yourself?

If the truth were told, most of us make a mess of being with sick people. Either we say too much, or we are so embarrassed that we don't mention the very things the ill person wants to talk about. The prayers we say are often hesitant and stumbling. People who are ill may have their work cut out reassuring and putting at their ease those of us who are trying to help them!

Many people feel awkward at the thought of being prayed over when the clergy or other members of their church visit them in hospital. I have a friend who was embarrassed when her minister stood by her hospital bed and prayed loud and long, just as the lunch-trolley was coming in. Apparently oblivious to the activity and smell of food around him, the pastor went on and on, eyes tightly shut. The nurse waved a plate of food at my friend and asked, by gesticulation, if she wanted any gravy. The food was cold by the time the prayer was finished.

Such a scenario is unusual. Hospital chaplains are sensitive to the needs of patients, and the vast majority of clergy come to be with you quietly, and do not impose themselves or their prayers on you.

It is precisely because they want to avoid causing embarrassment that many clergy wait to be asked before they pray with patients. If that happens, and you would like him or her to pray, do ask. It is sad to hear someone saying afterwards, "We had a good chat, but I would have liked a prayer."

Maybe we could do with the approach of a friend of mine who was vicar of a tough inner-city parish. He tells the tale:

I went to see an old wayfarer, George, in Ward 9. We talked a bit, and then I said, "Right, now I'm going to say a prayer."

George retorted, "Oh no you're not! I don't b***** well believe."

"Lie down and shut up," I replied. "God loves you whether you like it or not. You're not going to stop him!"

After I had prayed, he held my hand in both of his for a long time . . .

That, too, is unusual behaviour among the clergy! But it's a good story, and shows what can happen if barriers are overcome.

Receiving Holy Communion at home is another area that can cause concern, and this again is why some clergy wait to be asked. Many people feel so awkward at the prospect of the vicar seeing them in bed, that they think they could never concentrate properly on worshipping. But clergy are not embarrassed by this, any more than by the tears of the bereaved. Some are afraid of having to say responses on their own. Yet the clergy do not mind in the least if someone misses a response. (Most will probably say all the words themselves anyway.)

The fact that you have not attended church for a while need not prevent you from asking for Communion at home. Sometimes people who have drifted away from regular church attendance find that receiving the Sacrament at home sparks off a rediscovery of their faith.

Once they have experienced it, most people find a house-Communion far more relaxed and undemanding than they had expected. You don't have to sing hymns, stand up, kneel down or plough through long prayers for which you have not got the strength. My own experience of receiving Communion, both in hospital and at home, is of a gift, offered in an atmosphere of peace and gentleness. There is something healing in this alone.

"Part of something bigger" is a phrase I have often used in this book. It is particularly relevant when we are ill and other Christians are praying for us. Knowing that we are regularly remembered by individuals, groups and congregations draws us into the prayer of the whole body of Christ.

Monks and nuns, and especially those called to the

enclosed life of prayer, are there to hold the rest of us in the healing love of God. That is their job. So it is good to write (or ask a friend to write) and ask them to pray for you when you are sick, or facing any other sort of difficulty. This again helps you to realise that you are part of the on-going rhythm of worship which is the life-blood of the Church. Particularly when you are struggling, it helps to know that you are taken up into something which transcends space and time.

Tape-recordings of hymns and songs can deepen this sense that we belong to the wider Christian community. I find the tapes of music from Taizé particularly helpful here.[19]

* * *

Christ be with me, Christ within me,
Christ behind me, Christ before me,
Christ beside me, Christ to win me,
Christ to comfort and restore me.

Christ beneath me, Christ above me,
Christ in quiet, Christ in danger,
Christ in hearts of all that love me,
Christ in mouth of friend and stranger.
                    St Patrick (389–461).

Physical Pain

When we are in physical pain, the last thing we want to be told is that we should welcome it. Never mind how useful pain is to doctors in revealing what is wrong with us, or how close we ought to be feeling to Christ in his suffering, we wish to be rid of our misery.

So far I have looked at ways of praying which help to focus our minds away from our own ailments and onto God. That is important, but it is also essential to come to terms with our physical state, and to make that a part of praying too.

A most obvious and natural prayer is to ask God to free us from our suffering. There is no need to apologise to him for wanting relief; opening up our weakness is part of being ourselves and coming to God as his children. Although we may not receive from him the exact results we want, God always gives us himself when we pray like this, and is there with us, however hellish it all feels.

Some years ago, when I was suffering from a spate of bad headaches, my spiritual director advised me, "Make the pain your prayer." That was tough advice, but he was right. Following the principle of "protest and say Yes", we need both to voice our complaints to God, and to take on board what is happening to us.

I hesitate to write about this, because I have never suffered prolonged or intense pain, except when giving birth; and then it was somehow different, because there was an obvious purpose and an end in view. I cannot imagine what it must be like to endure constant, severe pain. But from experiences of headaches and back-trouble, I know that pain can be utterly draining, dominating all thought and feeling. So it is absolute sense to make the pain itself our offering to God; we have nothing else anyway.

On the rare occasions when I am immobilised and lying flat with a bad back, I never feel that I'm making much progress with prayer. But that's not the point. The spiritual life is not about being an "expert" in praying. What matters is that we keep looking in God's direction, rather than turning in on ourselves, which is one of the hazards of any sort of pain or illness.

* * *

"Lord, I give you my pain; it's yours too" is one prayer we can use, especially while looking at a figure of Christ on the cross. Or we can repeat a single name or word, such as "God", "Love", "Lord", or "Jesus", when we are hanging on to prayer by the skin of our teeth, as I have suggested before.

Nausea

Feeling sick is one of the deadliest enemies of prayer. Three queasy pregnancies taught me that! But even in the throes of a stomach-upset we can discover something about going into the misery with God, rather than trying to find God in spite of the misery.

One of the hardest kinds of illness to pray with is a common-or-garden tummy bug. You're not desperately ill; it is not a major crisis where you have to summon vast reserves of courage. But you feel absolutely *awful*.

On many days I have spent so long with my head in a bucket that I have hardly given God a thought, let alone managed any conscious praying. On other occasions I remember feeling pretty angry with God for letting sickness and diarrhoea into his creation. (To my shame, I am capable of getting more worked up about this than about the major diseases which ravage others.)

With my amateur knowledge of things biological, I know that we all need bacteria to survive, and that the bug which makes me ill is something to do with the conditions necessary for life. But this doesn't help much when I am feeling just plain sick.

So what about prayer? There will be the inevitable groaning and moaning to God, and asking to be relieved of this awful feeling. Then what? Anything more would seem to be an unreal proposition.

Nevertheless, two things do come to mind.

During one of my twenty-four-hour bouts of gastroenteritis, I tried putting a crucifix under my pillow. I wasn't sure how this would work out, but I found it surprisingly helpful. Lying in bed feeling dreadful, I could slip my hand up and get hold of the cross. This gave me an assurance that Jesus was there, in the physical misery, with me. He understood, he was close, and he could cope with my complaining and railing against God.

Something else that has become real to me when feeling

sick, is thinking about the fate of people in squalid refugee camps, who easily contract dysentery and similar diseases. I wonder what it must be like for them, being ill in a rough tent with no sanitation or running water?

On the wall downstairs I have a notice-board with names and pictures of people in various kinds of distress, such as famine, floods and political imprisonment. Looking at it is a form of intercession. When I am ill in bed I can think about those pictures, especially one of a forlorn family in a refugee camp in the Sudan, where hygiene is appalling, supplies scarce and the water filthy.

My lot is so different; and yet I have in common with the people who are sick in those camps this terrible feeling of nausea. So I pray with and for them, offering my comparatively tiny sufferings as a prayer for them in their great misery.

*   *   *

Lord, hang on to me, because I don't feel
well enough to hang on to you.

The Frustration and Humiliation

One of the many difficulties about being ill is that you can't get at all the things you long to do. Loss of independence is especially hard if you are at home with a young family, and cannot look after them. You feel as if your role and identity are being taken away from you.

Another frustration is that you have no energy to enjoy your favourite pastimes. Lacking the drive or enthusiasm to do much, your spirits become low, as well as your body.

This is a real test of your willingness to let go of dignity and achievement, and put your trust in God instead of yourself. You have nothing to offer him but your helplessness; this is hard, but it is a chance for prayer to be purified – less of you and more of God!

It is extremely difficult not to be irritable and critical when we are unwell and other people are doing what we would like to be doing ourselves. I have a job to control my temper when my back is playing up, and my long-suffering husband has to take over in the kitchen.

Self-pity is a stubborn demon to dethrone when we are ill. We think nobody understands, and we start to imagine that people resent having to do extra things for us. Either we don't have enough visitors, or people stay too long. "If so-and-so had been a little more thoughtful . . ." we say to ourselves.

In some ways self-centredness is unavoidable when you are ill. Whereas you would normally be busying yourself with work or domestic activities, much of your time and energy is now taken up with how you are going to cope, whether you have taken your pills, what the doctor will say next and when you will feel better. That is the agenda which has landed in your lap, and it is not your fault that so much of it concerns yourself.

There is also bound to be an element of loneliness during most long illnesses. Some people probably won't understand what you are going through; others will not be sympathetic for very long, and soon become more impatient than interested.

What we all have to watch, whether we have ear-ache or terminal cancer, is that we do not retreat into a miserable fortress of self, from which the only consolation is to shoot out barbed arrows at everyone in sight. Self-pity has to be seized by the scruff of the neck and given to God. He can deal with it, while we can't. When we ask for forgiveness, his mercy comes pouring out to meet us, and this is often the only thing that keeps us going.

The indignity of being unable to deal with one's own personal needs is another of the miseries endured by those with serious illnesses. A friend with multiple sclerosis puts this vividly:

> To be washed and dressed and even the most intimate details of one's toilet done by somebody else; someone else decides what and when you shall eat and drink, and puts the cup to your mouth . . . It takes every bit of humility you've got to stop screaming, "Will you not pour that down my neck as if it was a sewer!"

These words come from a talk that this friend gave, very bravely, at a seminar on healing. She then went on to make a crucial observation:

> Although I couldn't see it at the time, this is a share in our Lord's humility when he became man, and suffered the limitations and indignities of being human.

In facing her situation, my friend has found a way of coping which is neither a resigned giving-in, nor a grudging acceptance. She wholeheartedly loathes her illness, yet wholeheartedly takes it on board, and has discovered Christ alongside her in the process.

In the frustration of illness, the usual worldly values are turned upside-down. We are not productive, cost-effective people any more. We can *do* very little. And yet our value as human beings is not diminished. It can be a new experience to discover that we matter to God because we are who we are, and not because of what we can achieve.

* * *

Lord, this is intolerable.

I *am* grateful for all the help of people rallying round. I couldn't manage without them.

But I hate the fact that I need them. Teach me how to receive as well as give.

Help me to use this maddening situation positively, as a chance to let go of my desire to be organised, competent and always in control.

Set my spirit free, knowing that I am infinitely valuable to you, even when I'm stuck here!

I pray for all those people who never have the satisfaction of getting a good job done, because of permanent illness, or unemployment, or because they are struggling to scratch a frugal living under an unjust system. I pray for them, because I am — at least for the moment — one with them in this feeling of helplessness.

Jesus, I think of what they did to you in Jerusalem, stripping you of your clothes, nailing you to a cross. You have plumbed the depths of humiliation and weakness. You are in this with me, from the inside. I thank you for that.

We can be spiritually independent, even if physical independence is lost.

Dame Cicely Saunders[20]

In Great Suffering

I have a friend in a wheelchair, Anne, who developed muscular sclerosis after her husband committed suicide, leaving her with two young sons. Another friend, Mary, also with small children, suffers from a rare and debilitating tumour on the neck.

How do you pray in a situation like theirs? At one level I simply don't know. I have no idea what I would do if I were in their shoes. But getting to know them both has taught me a lot about relying on the grace of God.

They are both Christians. They have both gone through periods of darkness, when they couldn't think straight, pray consciously, or find anything positive to hang on to. And they have both shown tremendous courage.

Mary had radiotherapy, and was making a good recovery. But later on a further scan revealed that the tumour had not responded to the treatment, and was continuing to grow. She said that it was like being knocked down again when she had just begun to pick herself up. At this point she began to wonder if she could trust God any more. Paradoxically, it was a relief when she was able to acknowledge this, put it into words, and tell God how she felt.

Both my friends have been at rock-bottom. What they say about this speaks for itself (quoted with their permission):

Mary said, "I reached a point where I stopped holding on to God any more. But I have discovered that when I can't hold on to him, he is still holding on to me."

In a talk from which I also quoted in the previous section, Anne said:

God never anywhere promises to heal all our sickness, or magic away all our suffering. What He does promise, time and again, is *My grace is sufficient for you* (2 Corinthians 12:9). I find the implicatons of that promise mind-blowing. Living with chronic illness and disability, claiming that promise daily, has become the greatest challenge of my life . . .

. . . The result has been not happiness, not relief from pain,not ease, but joy. The deepest peace and satisfaction, wholeness and security, in knowing that God is in control of this outrageous and bloody situation. Knowing that He holds me in the palm of His hand, and that *nothing* can separate us.

She also wrote a song, which makes a powerful prayer:

My grace is all you need,
Today and every day,
My power will make you strong,
You need not be afraid.

My grace is all you need,
The saints have proved it true,
Through fire, torment and death,
They kept their faith in You.

My grace is all you need.
I claim Your promise now;
Without You at my side,
Life's a dark and lonely road.

My grace is all you need.
Sometimes almost too much,
As joy breaks through the pain
And I feel your healing touch.

My grace is all you need.
In temptation's darkest hour,
At the point of despair,
Then I know Your power.

My Lord, my God, my song
Shall never, never end,
And though death may be strong,
Your grace is all I need.

* * *

In a great affirmation of faith, after facing many discouragements and difficulties, St Paul wrote:

> *Who shall separate us from the love of Christ? Shall tribulation, or distress, or persecution? . . . No, in all these things we are more than conquerors, through him who loved us.*
>
> *For I am sure that neither death, nor life . . . nor things present, nor things to come, nor powers, nor height, nor depth, nor anything else in all creation, will be able to separate us from the love of God in Christ Jesus our Lord (Romans 8:35–39).*

We Are More Than Bodies

We are much more than the mass of cells that make up our bodies. Each person has depths of being and personality, memories, longings and creative gifts, which go far beyond the particular state their body happens to be in at any one moment.

Certainly our body, mind and spirit are intimately linked, and healing is concerned with all of those things. But the body is only a part of the whole person, and prayer transcends all bodily limitations.

When we pray for sick people, or for healing for ourselves, we are taken up into the energy of divine love which enfolds us as whole people. Wholeness in Christ is possible without a physically perfect body; and which of us has that anyway?

A friend from my schooldays, Hilary, whose story I often quote, suffered from the rare, muscle-wasting disease, myasthenia. Her body was a wreck. She lay paralysed except for her big toe; her tongue was hanging out, her eyes permanently closed. As an affectionate gesture, and to remind us that this was Hil, a young human being with a sweet nature and a sense of humour, the nurses used to manicure and varnish her finger-nails.

Hilary communicated with us by operating a highly sophisticated typewriter, "Possum", with her toe. Her conversation, which was always alert and often funny, would appear on a piece of paper at the other end of the small room. Mercifully she was not deaf, so we could talk to her freely. But it was an uncanny sensation when we spoke to her because we were tempted to address the typewriter, instead of the person whose head was on the pillow several feet away.

Her body gave no indication of life, apart from the mechanical heaving of her chest and the endless click of the ventilator. But the type-written page was full of her vitality and interest in the world around her.

When we prayed for her, we were holding in God's love not just a wasted body lying in bed, but somebody who remembered all about us, even though she couldn't see us; somebody who would invite us to look at photographs on the wall of her latest godchildren or nephews and nieces, even though she herself was blind; somebody who teased us ("Twerps!" once appeared on Possum's paper when we misunderstood the name of a German song she was talking about); somebody who was already whole, as a courageous and compassionate person; and somebody who remained faithful to God through all her devastating experience.

Hilary taught me something about all of us. God has

made us in his image, lovable and able to be loved. The person we are is not confined to our external appearance or bodily condition. Nor is prayer limited to outward, tangible things.

Another friend of mine, Steven, had a rare virus, which paralysed him for several months. In pain and unable to speak, he was immensely frustrated. Those of us who were praying for him realised that, even though the normal forms of human communication were impossible, the channel of prayer remained unimpaired. Intercession became a way of contact at a very deep level, a way of being with Steven and with God that transcended any physical blockage.

* * *

My father was dying of cancer some years ago, and knew it. During the final months of his life, my children sent him several home-made get-well cards. On one occasion my seven-year-old son had been learning at school about bones and the structure of the human body. So he decided to make a beautiful card for Grandpa, with a large picture of a skeleton on the front. When he showed me the finished article, I wondered if I could possibly give this to my father. It might have seemed terribly tactless! But, on reflection, I had a feeling it would be all right. So I took the card with me when I visited my father in hospital the next day.

He opened the card, looked at it carefully, and a large smile spread over his face, such as I had rarely seen since he became ill. And then he roared with laughter. "That's the best portrait I've had done for years!"

I was witnessing something profound beneath all the hilarity. There was a strange new freedom in my father, in spite of all his dreadful suffering. It was almost as if new life was beginning, a glimpse of resurrection in the middle of physical deterioration.

I believe that the prayer of a lot of people had something to do with this.

Facing the Truth

We are often afraid to face the truth, especially when someone is seriously ill. So we weave a web of lies around the sick person, adding deceit to deceit. This can lead to the sort of absurd situation I experienced as a teenager, when my mother was dying. Everyone knew, but no one could mention it. I would have given anything to cry freely with my mother, but the doctor would not allow it.

Fortunately things have changed since then. That was in the 1960s. More GPs do encourage families to grieve openly together now. This is harder in some ways, but at least you are living and praying with the pain of truth, not the pain of a lie.

Telling people about terminal illness has to be done gently and sensitively; some people need to come to terms with the truth a bit at a time; others want to know everything immediately. It is important that people should be given an honest answer, so that they can think and work through their situation openly with their families and with God.

Some people, however, refuse to face the truth; a lot

depends on how they are told, and how supported after receiving the news. I heard recently of a woman who was informed at an outpatient clinic that she had cancer. As soon as she stepped out of the hospital she convinced herself and her family that she was perfectly well. Even when her strength began to fail, she dismissed her illness as "nothing at all". Because she had put the shutters down on the truth, her family were drawn into the deception, and they never had the chance to share the pain or grow together during the last few months of her life.

In total contrast, an elderly clergyman preached a sermon in which he said, "Every night when I go to bed, I lie down and say, 'Into your hands, O Lord, I commend my spirit' – the words of Jesus when he died. I never know whether I'm going to wake up in the morning or not, so you could say I'm having a trial run!"

To be prepared for death is not a matter of being gloomy. On the contrary, readiness for death gives a lightness of touch, a care-free honesty about the fact that none of us can hold on to our earthly bodies and possessions for ever.

Death has become the great taboo in our society; it has replaced sex as the unmentionable subject. So people just switch off; they don't want to know.

But this is odd, since dying is the only experience we are all guaranteed to face. The whole idea of having to let go of what is familiar, and launch out alone into the unknown, appals many people. Prayer has an element of dying to self and uncertainty as well. Maybe if we prayed more we would fear death less, and be more ready for the intriguing "many mansions" which Jesus promised to prepare (John 14:2).

Facing the painful truth

In 1987 a woman whose son had died from Aids a year previously spoke on television. At first she had refused to believe he was dying, and had been closed up in bitterness. The first step towards facing the truth came when she could bring herself to rub her son's feet, legs and back, with a form of massage which is particularly comforting to people who are very sick with full-blown Aids.

When he died she swore she would never set foot in the hospital again. But then she realised that this would be to regress into her earlier refusal to face up to things. So she prayed to be given the courage to look squarely at what had happened.

She went on, 'To my surprise I found myself returning to the hospital. I was able to give leg-rubs to the lads with Aids, and show the other mums how to do it. This meant going back into the room where Maurice died. I nearly faltered then. But once I'd gone in, it was okay.'

She can now help the other mothers, because she understands what they are going through, and knows how they hide their own pain to spare their sons from blaming themselves.

She said, "I've learned that you can't walk around fear or pain; you've got to walk right through it. But it's hard, God knows."

And he does know, from the inside.

* * *

In this excerpt from Laurens Van der Post's novel, *A Story Like the Wind*,[21] the speaker is Ousie-Johanna, the family cook. She is complaining about her employer, Lammie, whose husband, Ouwa, has recently died. Lammie is pretending to be cheerful, and acting as if nothing tragic has happened. Ousie-Johanna says to the son of the family:

> *I don't know what is blerrie-well the matter with that Lammie of yours. Why has the good God in heaven given people grief if not to weep over it? Can't she see that she owes it to Ouwa to weep for him? If she's not careful she'll turn him into a ghost that will haunt us.*

New Values and Priorities

> *Facing illness and death, either in ourselves or in other people, can alter our values. Things which used to matter a lot pale into insignificance, and we become more aware of how vital human love and forgiveness are. We also start to appreciate ordinary things more fully, and see the beauty of the world with new eyes.*

"Live each day as if 'twere thy last," we used to sing solemnly at school assemblies. This line, from the old hymn *Awake My Soul*[22], seemed to me then rather morbid. But over the years I have come to see the wisdom in those archaic words.

A musical friend of our family regularly visits a children's hospice, and perches on the end of the beds playing her flute. Some of the children are well enough to play a variety of instruments, and parents quickly get involved in the fun of do-it-yourself concerts. In the middle of death, something comes alive. People discover new creativity and new ways of enjoying things together, because every moment is precious.

Illness can change our priorities. A friend of mine told me how she felt when her small son had an emergency operation. She had just been redecorating the house, and had been getting all hot and bothered about finding the right material for curtains and upholstery. Then her son had doubled up with stomach pains and was rushed into hospital for surgery. She said, "Since then I couldn't care less what colour the cushions are!"

Prayer is closely related to all this. Living contemplatively means being open to every present moment and aware of what matters most. It means being inwardly still and empty, in order to receive the full impact of creation; enjoying but not clinging, gazing but not grasping, living life to the full but dying to self.

We are all dying! But often it takes the closeness of somebody's death to make us appreciate the good things which are under our noses – the colours, the smells, the laughter, and the incredible fact that people love us.

Sometimes pain and illness break people, and there is no place for sentimentality about suffering. But tragedies can also become the seed-beds of new growth. If we ask God to make us more alive through the dark experiences, he will help us. The very fact that we want this to happen makes it possible.

* * *

If this were the last day of your life, ponder with God what you would look at, what you would savour, who you would like to be with, how you would listen to them, and with whom you would want to make peace.

Lord, I thank you for the way painful things can sharpen up the joy.

What Have We Done to Deserve This?

This is a common and understandable reaction to illness, bereavement and other misfortunes. "Why does disease have such power? Couldn't God have arranged things differently?" we ask. "Why should good and generous people suffer so much, while many selfish individuals appear to live in cheerful comfort?"

There are no simple explanations. Yet one thing is clear: logical standards of what is right and fair do not seem to correspond with the mysterious ways of God.

I recently heard of a couple who went through the rigorous interviews of adoption procedures, with the added strain of uncertainty over whether the baby's natural mother would finally relinquish the child. Eventually the process was complete and the baby was theirs. Two weeks later he died a cot death.

That couple must have felt like putting God on trial; it seemed so utterly meaningless and unfair.

We all feel like expressing our anger with God at times, and it is right that we should, as I have often said. When we do so, we may find ourselves asking what we have done to deserve such troubles. But we need to consider the implicatons of what we are saying when this word "deserve" creeps in.

Our question implies that we want an exact system of reward and punishment for all our behaviour. But take this to its logical conclusion. What would be our fate if we only got what we deserved? As the writer of Psalm 130 said, "If you, Lord, should note what we do wrong, who then could stand?" (verse 3). Fortunately the verse goes on: "But there is forgiveness with you." That is just as well!

If a system of absolute justice governed our fortunes, it is worth pondering what sort of scenario we would have. The only car-drivers to be killed would be the ones who had been dishonest or cruel to their families; God would only send rain on the land of virtuous farmers; and so on and so on. Yet Jesus himself pointed out that God is not like that: "He makes his sun rise on the evil and on the good, and sends rain on the just and on the unjust" (Matthew 5:45). If God is not like that, life in his world is not like that either.

What about the men, women and children who are ravaged by earthquake and famine? Have they directly "deserved" all their misery? If not, why should I, and not they, be rescued from suffering? If we are determined to apply it, the principle of "deserving" is a two-edged sword. In reality it is a non-factor. We are given and forgiven infinitely more than we deserve. That is the message of the gospel.

Maybe you have lived all your life for God, and a cruel

illness has hit you. You are not in the realm of reward and punishment. You are plunged into the heart of the mystery of suffering. All we have is the Cross – the unfairest thing of all – and the exuberant certainty of Jesus's disciples, ever since the first Easter, that he continues to be alive through and beyond all pain and death.

* * *

Job, who faced great anguish and misfortune, spoke these words:

> *I loathe my life;*
> *I will give free utterance to my complaint;*
> *I will say to God, Let me know why thou dost contend*
>   *against me.*
> *Thy hands fashioned and made me;*
>   *and now thou dost turn about and destroy me.*
>
> *Oh, that I knew where I might find God,*
>   *that I might come even to his seat!*
> *I would lay my case before him*
>   *and fill my mouth with arguments.*

The Lord answers Job out of a whirlwind:

> *Where were you when I laid the foundation of the earth?*
>   *Tell me, if you have understanding . . .*
> *Have you entered the storehouses of the snow?*
> *Is it by your wisdom that the hawk soars?*

Job replies:

I know that thou canst do all things,
  and that no purpose of thine can be thwarted.
Therefore I have uttered what I did not understand,
  things too wonderful for me, which I did not know.
      (Job 10:1–2, 8; 23:3–4; 38:4, 22; 39:26; 42:2–3).

How can you prove a man who leads,
To be a leader worth the following,
Unless you follow to the death? . . .
. . . I have to choose. I back the scent of life
Against its stink

G. A. Studdert Kennedy (1883–1929)
(Woodbine Willie)[23]

WEARINESS AND DEPRESSION

Letting the Side Down?

> "You're a Christian – things shouldn't get you down! Pull yourself together." Such bullying is both cruel and misguided. Who ever said that followers of Christ should be in a permanent state of happiness? Or that so-called "proper Christians" were never low or depressed?
>
> Jesus himself endured the deepest desolation imaginable, and men and women of God ever since have faced periods of darkness. We need a gentler approach.

Feeling weary and fed up is nothing to be ashamed of. We have to treat ourselves as gently as God does. We need in fact to "love ourselves". This idea can appear suspect, as if we are pandering to self-pity or condoning our own evil. But loving ourselves is accepting the truth that we are of infinite value to God, however unlovable we may feel. It is often pointed out that Jesus told us to love our neighbours *as ourselves*, and never said that we should hate ourselves.

When life is hell, your best friends stick by you. They listen, they understand and they take you seriously. They don't make you feel guilty or chide you for feeling the way you do. As a result, you are completely free to tell them exactly how things are. They may gently help you to see what your hurt and unhappiness are doing to you. But they will love you through it all.

God is like that. The prophet Hosea sees him as a father, tenderly teaching a small child to walk, and picking him up when he falls over (Hosea 11:1–4). Elsewhere God is described as a mother-hen sheltering her chicks beneath her wings (Psalm 91:4, Matthew 23:37).

Depression makes us acutely aware of our own nothingness, so we have no alternative in prayer but to reach out to God in sheer dependence. The point where our own resources run out is the point where his begin, and we have to hang on to him through thick and thin.

Praying when we are low in spirits does not necessarily make us feel better. But by doggedly continuing to say, "Lord, I am yours," or "Jesus, help me," or some such phrase, our low feeling has at least become part of prayer, rather than something which is keeping us away from God.

The journey through darkness is one that we share with Christ, although it takes an act of sheer faith to affirm that. Even he experienced Godlessness, in a moment of desolation on the cross that we can hardly begin to fathom: "My God, my God, why have you forsaken me?" (Matthew 27:46). Jesus has already descended into hell. We are not alone, even though it may feel like it.

* * *

Lord, now thou has reduced me to nothing,
I wait on Thee to make something of me.
I don't know what.
You have brought me so low, there is nothing I want to
    do or be,
    but I wait on Thee.

Richard Harries[24]

Prayer can flow into music, and music can enter prayer,

as a channel of God's healing power. King Saul in the Old Testament was relieved of dark and melancholy moods when David played the harp to him (1 Samuel 16:14–23). One way of praying when we feel low is to play something gentle and beautiful, like the slow movement of Mozart's 3rd Violin Concerto (K299), and to read a passage at the same time, such as this:

My steadfast love shall not depart from you . . .
  says the Lord, who has mercy on you.
O afflicted one, storm-tossed, and not comforted . . .
With everlasting love I will have compassion on you,
  says the Lord your Redeemer.

(Isaiah 54:8, 10–11)

I have loved you with an everlasting love;
I will restore health to you,
  and your wounds I will heal, says the Lord.
I will satisfy the weary soul,
  and every languishing soul I will replenish.

(Jeremiah 31:3; 30:17; 31:25)

Other possible music includes:

Brahms: Violin Concerto in D. 1st movement.
Brahms: German Requiem. Especially the 5th movement with chorus and soprano: *Thee I will comfort as one whom his mother comforts (Ich will euch trösten, wie einen seine Mutter tröstet).*
Fauré: Requiem, especially the *Sanctus* and *Pie Jesu.*
Mozart: Andante for flute and orchestra in C. K315.

Mozart: Concerto for flute and harp. K299. 2nd movement.
Mozart: Clarinet Quintet in A. K581. 2nd movement.
Mozart: Piano Concerto in C. No. 21. K467. 2nd movement.
Mozart: Clarinet Concerto in A. 2nd movement.
(Most of the second movements are slow and meditative; it can be especially therapeutic to play on, to the livelier third movements.)

Some people are helped by songs and choruses such as: "Jesus Christ, One with God" and "The Lord my Shepherd", on *Jesus Praise*[25]; also "For You are my God" on *Come and Worship*, with the choir of St Michael-le-Belfry, York.[26]

Depression

As I write this, I am not feeling depressed. But there have been times in the past when I have sunk very low in spirits. I remember how difficult it was to relate to the kindly advice given to me by people who hadn't a clue what I was feeling. Only those who spoke out of their own experience of darkness could help.

So I have looked up my old journals, to see what I wrote during the bouts of mild depression that I suffered some years ago. I reproduce some extracts in the hope that first-hand thoughts, struggles and prayers, which were then intended for no eyes but my own, may give some hope to anyone who is feeling depressed now.

This awful, dull ache round the solar plexus . . .

I alienate the people I love most. I'm prickly about everybody's response to me. I dread meeting anyone outside, and I resent any demands made on me.

I know I irritate and hurt people. I can see how it happens, but I can't stop it. It's as if I need to vent my feelings on someone – or something.

I'm getting upset over such trivial things. But what aches inside isn't just these immediate things; it goes much deeper. It feels like a swamp of misery underneath . . .

I must resist the temptation to cut people by words or unkind silences. I must open up my wounds to Christ.

Don't stand still. You are journeying through a desert, and your survival depends on your determination to keep moving.

This entry comes some months later:

Back again in this heavy cloud. Each time the stripping seems to be more painful.

After a talk with Father N., I do believe this can be used, as intercession for other people going through hell – and in some sort of dying to self.

I need to be more quiet with God. Pour out my darkness into the love which is streaming from the cross, like a Carmelite in silent adoration of Christ crucified.

Offer it all to God, so that he can transform and take up my pain into his redemptive suffering in the world.

Lord, I plunge into you, and I bring my depression with me. I'm giving you the depression because it's all I've got to offer at the moment. It's still mine, I'm still feeling it – but it's yours as well . . .

It feels as if everyone loathes me. But people's opinions of me can't hurt me without my consent. I WILL not be ruled by the desire for approval, which gets blown up out of all proportion when I'm like this.

What matters most? My own ego doesn't matter a scrap. Yet it's my ego that lurches around when I feel like this, colouring everything I do with insidious self-pity.

Lord, free me from this tyrant of self.

I don't matter.

Yet I do matter to you. You love me. There's freedom in that.

Lord, let me be God-possessed,
                love-possessed,
                instead of self-possessed.

From the following year:

Empty, miserable and dreary.

Heavy and lifeless.

In the darkness with God.

God is more than darkness. Life is more than this.

. . . This depression is like a huge wave. Lord, help me
to
ride on it: don't let it engulf me.
However awful I feel, nothing can stop me praying,
  nothing can stop me loving,
    unless I freely choose to let that happen.

Operation depression:

1. Face it squarely
2. Pour it all out before the Cross
3. Keep very still
4. Abandon everything I am to God
5. Look Jesus in the eye
6. Stop self-hatred – he loves me
7. No more rushing to the biscuit-tin
8. Do something practical, and endure the pain like toothache.

Next day:

This is hard work. Much easier to slump back into a cushion of misery.

* * *

Lord, give me strength for the effort of each moment as it comes.

Gifts

One of the most wretched effects of depression is that we lack the energy or initiative to do anything, respond to anyone, or enjoy any part of God's world. Being told to "snap out of it" only makes matters worse.

Yet there is something we can do ourselves in the battle against inertia. This is to make the effort (not easy!) to look at and listen to the things immediately around us. If we can do this, new possibilities open up for God to touch and help us when misery looms large, often through the smallest fragments of his creation.

The great Dutch Christian, Corrie ten Boom, was held in solitary confinement in the Nazi concentration camp at Ravensbruck during the Second World War, because she and her family had given shelter to Jews. In her cell she found immense comfort, even joy, in the presence of an ant. It was another living thing, made by God as she was.

I had almost put my foot where he was one morning as I carried my bucket to the door, when I realised the honour being done me. I crouched down and admired the marvellous design of legs and body. I apologised for my size, and promised I would not so thoughtlessly stride about again.

After a while he disappeared through a crack in the floor. But when my evening piece of bread appeared on the door shelf, I scattered some crumbs, and to my joy he popped out almost at once. He picked up a heroic piece, struggled down the hole with it, and came back for more. It was the beginning of a relationship.[27]

Most of us do not face that sort of persecution. But Corrie's experience can help us when we are going through a period of low spirits. If we are alert, a similar gift of hope may land at our feet.

This idea could easily sound twee and sentimental: "If you're down in the dumps, all you have to do is look at the birds and the bees, and you'll feel just fine!"

"Yuk!" is all I can say to that.

In the first place, it takes a considerable effort of will to come out of ourselves and appreciate the natural world when we are down in spirits.

Secondly, enjoying nature will not automatically make us feel ten times better. Yet we will find a new ingredient added to our experience, if we can summon the energy to be attentive to the natural world.

I once made a list of things I have tried to hang on to, in the struggle to counterbalance the misery of depression. I don't expect that everyone else will find delight in the same things; my aim is simply to give an illustration of what I have been saying.

A smooth pebble, picked up on the beach, with the most beautiful shape and colour.

The cat's soft fur and long tail.

Van Gogh's painting of a lark above a cornfield.

The shape and texture of – yes! – a cauliflower.

The flame-like leaves of trees in autumn.

The smell of good soap, particularly a kind I often use which is made by blind people.
Pink and apricot sunsets.
The song of the chaffinch and the willow warbler.

No doubt, if someone had said to me, "You ought to look at this or listen to that," I would have replied, "Oh, yes," but remained dull and closed inwardly. Depression makes us perverse, so that we are unwilling to take ideas from anyone else, however good they may be; we have to discover things for ourselves.

God deals with each of us differently. All that is asked of us is to be ready and open to receive what he offers us, here and now. This means making space around the particular things which catch our attention – not forcing anything, but just seeing what happens.

* * *

Sometimes looking at lovely things can actually increase our pain. Veteran soldiers have said how the beautiful wild flowers in France added to their sense of the futility of war.

But for someone like Mother Julian of Norwich, the great fourteenth-century English mystic, creation's small things give an assurance of the eternal love of God. She too lived at a time of upheaval and darkness:

And he showed me more, a little thing, the size of a hazelnut, on the palm of my hand, round like a ball. I looked at it thoughtfully and wondered, "What is this?" And the answer came, "It is all that is made." I marvelled that it continued to exist and did not suddenly disintegrate; it was so small. And again my mind supplied the answer, "It exists, both now and for ever, because God loves it." In short, everything owes its existence to the love of God.[28]

Are we willing to:

See with our eyes,
hear with our ears,
understand with our hearts,
and turn and be healed?
     (Based on Isaiah 6:10)

Tired

When we are worn out, and our own resources are close to nil, the only prayer possible is simply to let go into God. Exhaustion brings into focus our inner poverty and total dependence on him. Relying on ourselves is no longer a temptation; it's an impossibility.

There are, of course, different kinds of tiredness.

There is an exhilarating kind, which you can experience when things are going well at work, or in certain meetings and conferences. Busy family events can have the same effect, so that you are riding on the crest of a wave, tired but happy. Then prayer is not so much an offering of weariness as of thankfulness.

Such exhilaration, however, is usually followed by fatigue. I remember a parish residential weekend, where we had very little sleep the first night because of over-excited children and strange beds. The next day went well, but breakfast on the final morning saw many of us with tired and befuddled brains. I wondered how on earth I was going to be able to lead my group. But a wise friend pointed out to me that a "theology of tiredness" is a gateway to trust in God. Does it all depend on us?!

Another kind of tiredness comes when life is going badly: people are difficult, work is draining, or you have personal problems to contend with. Then your resilience is low, and you are liable to explode if someone is awkward or does not understand.

The invitation of Jesus to lose your life in order that you may find it (Mark 8:35) takes on a new dimension when you are as tired as this. You are so worn out that you have nothing within yourself to draw on. Prayer means surrendering yourself into God's hands and losing your strength and ability in his. All you can offer is your emptiness.

At such times, short prayers, like "Jesus: my weakness into your strength", are invaluable.

Perhaps the commonest type of tiredness is a mixture of happiness and weariness. We are busy with numerous commitments, and enjoy being involved in so many things. But if fatigue and the pressure of demands get the better of us, we snap. This tends to happen when we would least want it.

About half past seven in the evening is a time in our house when the children are tired and most need me to be patient and responsive. My own resources are often at a low ebb at this point in the day, and my temper easily frayed. Then the only way I can pray is to say under my breath, "Lord, this is yours", or "Jesus, live in me". I cannot handle my weariness and the chaos around me on my own; all I can do is give the whole situation to him.

* * *

Why are you so full of heaviness, my soul;
and why so unquiet within me?
O put your trust in God:
for I will praise Him yet
who is my deliverer and my God (Psalm 42:5–6).

PROBLEMS WITH TIME

No Time for Quiet

> *It can be most frustrating to have no solitude, and little opportunity for quiet prayer. But the very fact that we wish there was more time to pray reveals our inner desire for God; and that is important, because reaching out to him is the heart of praying.*
>
> *Maybe all we have to offer him at this particular point is our lack of time. Even this can become a prayer of wanting God, or a "dart of longing love", to use the classic phrase.*[29]

You are tired and over-worked and you have a headache. People are being awkward, interruptions abound, and you long to be organised and have some peace. Frustration like this makes God seem pretty remote.

We are all tempted to see demands and chores as irritations to be "got through", so that we can then start really living, praying and doing God's work. The busier we are, the more we tend to think like this. It is interesting how often the word "just" keeps cropping up: "I'll *just* do these jobs before I start thinking about God"; "Let me *just* get through this difficult patch and then I'll be able to concentrate on being a Christian again." What we are doing is building escape-routes out of the present moment into some imaginary ideal future haven that we will never reach.

But we have nothing but the present moment, and it is here that God is waiting for us. Everything we do can be given to God, and there are no exceptions.

We can accept all that in theory. But it is tough if we

have pressures of work, lively children, visitors staying and a garden full of weeds. If we are honest, living prayerfully is an ideal towards which we are moving, rather than a goal we usually achieve. But there are some things which can help us to come closer to that vision.

One is to make a deliberate act of consecration of the whole day to God in the morning. Then it's done, whether or not we remember his presence later on.

It can also be helpful to identify some sort of sign or object as a symbol of our basic desire to live all our life rooted and grounded in God. One of my favourites is a Celtic cross on a chain, which I wear as a necklace. Another is an icon of Jesus. Such a picture, painted with prayer and fasting, points beyond itself to Christ who is present with me throughout the day.

Water is another great symbol of Christ. I know someone who uses the prayer, "Living Water, cleanse me, and be a spring of eternal life welling up within me," when she first turns the tap on in the morning. As I have often said, another invaluable companion during the day is a single word or phrase. One prayer which comes to my rescue if I am harassed and feel like tearing my hair is, "Lord, this is yours". I like this prayer because it is deliberately ambiguous. The word "yours" can mean "coming from you" or "given to you", and I want to express both those things.

There will never be time to *do* very much! What gets done depends on the opportunities and resources which God gives us in any case. But there will always be time to pray, because all time can be prayed in.

I know of a man, whom I will call Martin, who is a night nurse in a geriatric hospital. When he comes home he is exhausted, and, even after a sleep, finds it a struggle to do essential things with his family and round the house. He is a Christian, and involved in many things at church as well.

At one time he was depressed because he wanted to come closer to God, but felt that his prayer-life was a shambles. He managed five minutes with a Bible passage most days, but tiredness and other pressures seemed to prevent any more.

He described what it was like at night during the long hours on duty:

> Sometimes a dozen things happen at once and it's bedlam; but there are long stretches when it's very still and quiet. I do feel near to God then. You're close to life and death, and there's something awesome about that. I often feel that God is there when someone is dying.
>
> Sometimes it's awful – the mess and the smells, and some old people can be very crotchety. But I try to do the work for God even when I'm hating it.

Martin was relieved at the suggestion that God was not wanting to put extra burdens onto an already highly demanding life. Perhaps God actually wanted him to *relax* when he came home, worn out from work. Martin began to realise that God was already giving him a great deal of material for prayer in the ward at night: intercession, silence and sharing of the world's pain. His task was to respond to what was already there, not to hunt around for further disciplines to impose upon himself.

Days off work were different; there were chances for other kinds of praying then. But in the hospital Martin only had to recognise the possibilities for prayer which were under his nose.

* * *

Many ancient Celtic prayers capture the essential truth that all of life is God's life and contained in his love, and that every activity can become prayer. The hymns and prayers interweave mundane and heavenly things with a disarming simplicity. In her booklet *God under my Roof*[30] Esther de Waal quotes some poems sung by women in the mornings:

> *I will kindle my fire this morning*
> *In the presence of the holy angels of heaven . . .*
> *God kindle Thou in my heart within*
> *A flame of love to my neighbour . . .*

Another is a farmer's prayer:

> *I will go out to sow the seed,*
> *In the name of Him who gave it growth . . .*

There are also many journey-prayers, for example:

> *Bless to me, O God*
> *The earth beneath my foot,*

Bless to me, O God,
  The path whereon I go.

Life is only for loving. Time is only that we may find God.
St Bernard

Too Much To Do

Either you fight against a demanding schedule, or you surrender into the flow of it. Constant demands can seem like a treadmill, dreary and draining. But by positively accepting every task and interruption as it comes, you can become less bound by the sense of compulsion. A job that was forcing itself on you becomes something you freely do, the object of your whole-hearted attention.

Saying "Yes" to what is required in the present moment can be a kind of dying to self. Plans for a peaceful evening have to take second place to the needs of other people; the desire for a clean and tidy house must wait, while we seize an opportunity to be quiet with God. Or we may have to abandon our time of quiet and solitude with God, in order to deal with an urgent demand.

Letting go of the many other things we would like to be doing and giving all our attention to the task in front of us is a positive act of limitation, for love's sake. It is a form of obedience, just as real as a vow in a monastery or convent.

Decide and do

Sometimes there is so much to do that we wonder which job to tackle first, and when we should take a break. It would be so much easier if God would tell us what to do, step by step, so that we could simply obey without thinking.

Praying and agonising about each decision can become ridiculous. The motto "decide and do" is useful. I find it best to survey the possibilities as quickly as I can, offer my will to God, and then get on and choose, doing my best to let go of preoccupations with other things on the list.

A positive view of incompleteness

The completion of jobs and projects can become an obsession. We forget that the present moment is never complete. If I am sowing seeds I cannot harvest the vegetables at the same time. I can, however, be wholly given to the particular part of the process in which I am involved today.

Prayer, too, is always incomplete, because it is a longing for God, not a possessing of him. We are always journeying into a deeper relationship with him. We have never *done* our praying, in the same way that we have finished our exams or done the decorating. So our frustration when we have to curtail a prayer-time in order to go to work or cook a meal can be made into a shaft of desire for God, which is itself a particularly valuable part of praying.

* * *

Peace must always exist in the midst of our imperfections . . .
Imitate the calm of the sailor standing on the deck of his ship.
                                                  Abbé de Tourville[31]

Lord, You put twenty-four hours in a day;
You gave me a body which gets tired and can only do
so much.
Show me what You want me to do,
    and how You want me to pray.
Help me to
    Open my eyes and look;
    Taste what I am eating;
    Listen to what I am hearing;
    Face what I am suffering;
    Celebrate the ways I am loved;
    And offer what I am doing,
So that the water of the present moment
    may be turned into wine.

Insomnia and a Rosary

When you cannot sleep, you have too much time on your hands
rather than too little! Insomnia is a beast, because the harder you
try to fall asleep, the less likely you are to do so. Seeing sleepless-
ness as a friend, a chance to pray, instead of as an enemy, is one
way of coping.

Many hours spent lying awake have taught me the futility

of trying to get to sleep by sheer will power. I have now come to see sleepless periods as an opportunity to give some space to God which might not be possible during busy days, and I have worked out my own way of praying in bed during these night hours. Looking at my particular pattern may spark off ideas in other people who want to do something positive with their insomnia. We need to experiment and see what is best for us.

I lie flat on my back and use a rosary[32], with my own version of the traditional mysteries or themes associated with this aid to prayer. The beads give me something to hang on to, literally, in the bleak loneliness of the early hours.

First I take hold of the cross at the end of the rosary, and say – or, rather, think to myself – the ancient "Jesus Prayer" which has been used for centuries in the Orthodox churches: "Lord Jesus Christ, Son of God, have mercy on me a sinner." Then, with each bead between the cross and the central medallion, I simply say the name, "Jesus".

The small medallion has on it a tiny figure of Mary with Jesus as a baby. I hold this and ponder the miracle of the Incarnation, saying part of the opening of St John's Gospel:

In the beginning was the Word;
And the Word was with God, and the Word was God.

219

And the Word became flesh and dwelt among us,
Full of grace and truth.

The main part of the rosary is divided into five sets of ten beads, and there is a larger bead between every set.

With each of the first ten beads, I say the words of Mary from Luke 1, when she received the astounding news that she would bear the Son of God: "Behold the servant of the Lord; be it unto me according to your word." At the back of my mind while I say this are the words of the German mystic, Meister Eckhart: "The eternal birth must take place in you." Saying those words of Mary, many times, is a powerful way of offering myself to God in the darkness.

I often pause for a short or long time between the beads. There is a peacefulness in prayer at night which is quite different from any other time.

With the second set of ten beads I remember Jesus's active ministry of teaching and healing. I picture him in the hills above Capernaum, and round the shores of the Sea of Galilee, surrounded by people. With each bead I pray, "Jesus, Lord, come to my aid."

With the third set of beads, I move on to pondering Jesus's suffering and death, and with every bead I say again the "Jesus prayer": "Lord Jesus Christ, Son of God, have mercy on me a sinner."

The fourth set of beads represents Jesus' resurrection, and for this I use the prayer of Thomas, "My Lord and my God." Thomas was desolate and full of doubt after the crucifixion, but when he saw the risen Jesus for himself, he used these words in his tremendous joy and relief (John 20:28).

With the final ten beads, I make an act of faith that Jesus will give me the strength and resources to cope with the coming day. I pray, "Jesus live in me."

This brings me back to the medallion, from which I return to the cross, saying the name "Jesus" with each bead.

Sometimes I go through the rosary more than once. At other times I find I have fallen asleep before I reach the end!

Sleepless nights are not the only occasions when one can pray in this way. A rosary can also be helpful on long journeys, during illness, while waiting in queues, or, indeed, at any time.

* * *

Rosary Prayers:

Lord Jesus Christ, Son of God, have mercy on me a sinner (said with the crucifix)

And the Word became flesh (said with the medallion)

Behold the servant of the Lord; be it unto me according to your word (ten beads)

Jesus, Lord, come to my aid (ten beads)

Lord Jesus Christ, Son of God, have mercy on me a sinner (ten beads)

My Lord and my God (ten beads)

Jesus, live in me (ten beads)

I'm Not Sure if I Want to Pray!

When ten or twenty minutes fall into our lap, God is offering us a gift. Nobody wants our attention, no commitment requires our presence, and no task is urgent. We actually have a space in which we could sit still and be alone with God. This is a real test of priorities. Are we willing to let go of all the other things we would like to be doing?

There are many reasons why we sometmes feel reluctant to pray. We may be pulled by a half-decorated bedroom or an unopened newspaper. Or we may be tempted to escape into busyness because we are afraid of what God might demand of us. Then we are saying "No" to prayer because we do not want to be too exposed to him, too vulnerable to the cost of discipleship.

But God never asks the impossible of us. He only draws us towards what we are capable of doing. In other words, he enables us to become our real selves – and to find true happiness.

When we do settle down to spend time with God, we may have to start by offering him our very reluctance to pray, if that is all we bring with us! It is not easy suddenly to change gear in the middle of a hectic day, and our minds will probably rattle on with numerous distractions. That doesn't matter as long as we stay put.

On a practical level, I again find it helpful to use a candle, as a way of saying to God, "This flame won't go out. It is a sign that I *want* to be open to you all the way through this period of time, even though I may wander off into a buzz of mental activity." Repeating a prayer such as, "Spirit of Jesus, breathe on me", is a way of moving into the stillness which is always there, underneath the noise which daily life usually imposes upon it.

A good prayer when using a candle is to ask Christ to melt us into himself, so that we may become increasingly absorbed into the love and silent presence of God our Father.

Many Christians will agree that the more we make space for God, the more he makes himself known to us.

* * *

Anyone who prays knows the connection between the "Yes" which is expressed and, to some extent, diluted in the affairs of daily life, and the "Yes" spoken neat in prayer.
Maria Boulding[33]

Jesus said, "Be like men who wait for their master's return from a wedding-party, ready to let him in the moment he arrives and knocks. Happy are those servants whom the master finds on the alert when he comes" (Luke 12:36–37, *NEB*).

Epilogue in Canterbury

Buried in the rubble of a street in Canterbury for eleven hundred years was a small cross which looks like this.

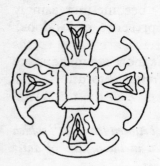

The way each arm of the cross opens right out can be seen as a symbol of all our praying in the shadows.

The upward movement represents our reaching out to God in trust, opening our whole being to him, often in emptiness and darkness.

Into your hands, O Lord, I commend my spirit (Psalm 31:5).

The downward thrust stands for God's pervading the hidden depths of our being. It also conveys our need to be rooted and grounded in God, come what may.

In him we live and move and have our being (Acts 17:28).

The cross beams stand for our experience of the world. The more we pray, the more exposed we become to the pain of other people, and aware of God's activity in and through suffering, both in our everyday life and in the wider world. Prayer also opens our eyes to the miracle of creation.

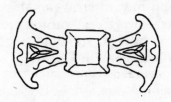

Each arm opens out eventually into infinity, the unfathomable, silent presence of God who is in and beyond all things.

God is also at the centre of the cross, in Jesus, who entered the heart of all our sin and misery, and redeemed it from the inside.

So this Canterbury cross can be a symbol of all our praying and longing and suffering with God.

On the four small triangles on each beam, there is a typically interwoven Celtic pattern. This is a reminder of the intimate connection between the things of God and

225

everyday life, a link which is reflected, as we have seen, in much Celtic poetry (see pp. 166–7).

Thomas Becket, Archbishop of Canterbury, stood in his cathedral on 29 December 1170, and turned to face the knights as they burst in to murder him.

This was his supreme "Yes", a "Yes" to death, but also a "Yes" to God's life in him. It was a "Yes" reached through prayer and inward struggle, an acceptance made possible by Christ's own "Yes" on the cross.

Somehow we too have to stand still, face our shadows, and become pain-bearers with Christ.

Peace,
These things had to come to you and you accept them;
This is your share of the eternal burden,
The perpetual glory.

(Words of Thomas Becket to the distraught women of Canterbury just before his death)[34]

NOTES

INTRODUCTION

1. Quoted in *The Lord of the Journey* ed. Pooley and Seddon (Collins, 1986), p. 351.

PART 1. Hurts

1. *Marked For Life* (SPCK/Triangle, 1985), pp. 63–4.
2. Source unknown.
3. "Little Gidding" 1.206, *Four Quartets* (Faber, 1970).
4. *Yes to God* (DLT, 1975), ch. 3, p. 50.
5. In *The Oxford Book of Prayer*, ed. George Appleton, OUP, 1988.
6. Constance Babbington Smith, *Iulia de Beausobre: A Russian Christian in the West* (DLT, 1983) p. 134; also referred to in Iulia de Beausobre *Creative Suffering* (Fairacres Publication No 88, 1984), pp. 16–17.
7. Quoted in *Lord of the Journey*, ed. Pooley and Seddon (Collins, 1986), p. 349.
8. *Letter from Taizé*, May – June 1986.
9. *The Listener*, 24 October 1946, p. 555.
10. Adapted from a prayer by Jim Cotter, in *Prayer at Night*, 4th edn (Cairns Publicaton, 1988), p. 50.
11. These words were found scribbled on a note-pad on the desk of a parish priest, soon after his death.
12. Translated from the Russian, in *Pencil Letter* (Bloodaxe Books, 1988).
13. Prue Wilson, *My Father Took Me to the Circus* (DLT, 1984), p. 22.
14. CMS magazine, *Yes*, May–June 1988.

PART 2. Praying With your Own Sinfulness

1. Available on *Your Hundred Best Tunes*, New Chart, vol 3, Decca SPA 565 (or cassette KCSP 565).
2. See also the music for praying with low spirits on page 201.

3. Record MS003/EE1.
4. From St Michael le Belfry, WST C9686.

5. *The English Poems of George Herbert*, ed. C. A. Patrides (Everyman/Dent, 1974), p. 192.
6. Gerard Hughes, *God of Surprises*, (DLT, 1985), p. 117.
7. Iago to Othello, *Othello* Act III, iii. 1. 169 (Collins, 1968).
8. Source unknown.
9. Roald Dahl, *James and the Giant Peach* (Puffin, 1961), pp. 32–33.
10. *Thoughts in Solitude* (Burns & Oates, 1987), p. 24.
11. Philippa Craig, *Living from Within* (Grail, 1979), p. 22.
12. In Leslie Houlden (ed.), *A Celebration of Faith* (Hodder & Stoughton, 1970), p. 200.
13. From *Prayer is my Life* (USPG, no date).
14. *Praying Round the Clock* (Mowbray, 1983), p. 105.
15. (Fairacres Publication No 88) pp. 13–14.
16. This idea of reducing a text to certain key phrases and words is fully explored in *Towards Contemplation. A Practical Introduction for Prayer Groups*, by Peter Dodson (Fairacres Publication No 64); see also his *Contemplating the Word* (SPCK).
17. "Silence in Prayer: the Meaning of Hesychia" in M. Basil Pennington (ed.), *One Yet Two: Monastic Tradition East and West* (Cistercian Studies Series No 29), p. 31.
18. Quoted by Sr Edmée in Silence in *Prayer and Action* (Fairacres Publication No 78).
19. *Listening to God and Listening to Community* (Fairacres Publication No 69).
20. On a Christmas card, adapted from a prayer by the late Bishop of Bloemfontein.

PART 3. Misfortunes, Fears and Frustrations

1. *A Doorway to Silence* (DLT, 1968), p. 3.
2. Father William Barry, "Wrestling with God", *The Tablet* 11 April 1987.
3. Ibid.
4. From *Heiligenstadt Testament* (1802), translated by Alfred Kitchin.
5. *Seeds of Contemplation* (Anthony Clarke Books, 1961), p. 204–6.
6. *Moment of Christ* (DLT, 1984), p. 62.
7. (SPCK, 1983), pp. 10–11.
8. From a prayer card by Spes Sancta, Newbury.
9. *Thoughts in Solitude* (Burns & Oates, 1975), p. 21.
10. Talking on BBC Television, The Cost of Discipleship, February, 1988.
11. *Heaven in Ordinary* (Mayhew McCrimmon, 1985).

12. *Praying Round the Clock* (Mowbray, 1983), p. 54.
13. For more information about Soviet Christians in prison contact "The Vigil", c/o Rev Dr Dick Rogers, 63 Meadow Brook Road, Birmingham B31 1ND.
14. *Oxford Book of Prayers* edited by George Appleton, p. 284.
15. From *Prayer Is My Life* (USPG).
16. Dom John Chapman, *The Spiritual Letters* (Sheed & Ward, 1938), p. 25.
17. The prayers are to be found on pages 9 and 25. The motifs are on pages 9 and 15. Published by Triangle, 1985.
18. David Adam, *The Edge of Glory* (SPCK/Triangle, 1985), p. 49; the motif is on p. 87.
19. For example, TZ 405 *Cantate*, TZ 408 *Resurrexit*. Production by Presses de Taizé (distributed by Auvidis).
20. BBC Radio 4 "Sunday" 27 September, 1987.
21. (Penguin, 1972), p. 436.
22. Written by Bishop Thomas Ken (1637–1711).
23. From the poem "Faith" in *The Unutterable Beauty* (Hodder & Stoughton, 1964).
24. *Praying Round the Clock* (Mowbray, 1983), p. 101.
25. Day Spring Record DAY 4018 (or cassette TC-DAY 4018).
26. Record No. MS003/EE1.
27. *The Hiding Place* (Hodder & Stoughton, 1971), p. 144.
28. *Revelations of Divine Love*, ch. 5, translated by Clifton Wolters (Penguin, 1966).
29. Anon., *The Cloud of Unknowing*, translated by Clifton Wolters (Penguin, 1961), ch. 6.
30. (Fairacres Publication No 87), pp. 13, 18, 17.
31. *Letters of Direction* (Dacre Press, Westminster, 1961), p. 81.
32. Robert Llewelyn, in his small book, *A Doorway to Silence* (DLT, 1986), has many insights and suggestions about the use of a rosary.
33. *Marked for Life* (SPCK/Triangle, 1985), p. 5.
34. From the play, *Murder in the Cathedral* by T. S. Eliot (Faber, 1965), Part II, line 246ff.

Acknowledgments

I am grateful, to Father William Barry SJ for permisson to refer to his article "Wrestling with God" in *The Tablet*; also to Clare Amos for permission to quote her article about weeping and prayer in the CMS magazine *Yes*; to Dame Cicely Saunders, DBE, for permission to quote two extracts from a BBC Radio 4 "Sunday" interview, 27 September 1987; to Dr Jean Vanier, for permission to quote his interview on the BBC television programme "*The Cost of Discipleship*", in February 1988; to the Rev David Adam for permission to use the motifs from his book *The Edge of Glory*; and to the Dean of Canterbury Cathedral for permission to use the Canterbury Cross in the Epilogue.

Thanks are due to the following for permission to quote from copyright sources:

Anthony Clarke Books, 16 Garden Court, Wheathampstead, Herts AL4 8RF, for the extract from *Seeds of Contemplation* by Thomas Merton, 1961.

BBC Publications, 35 Marylebone High Street, London W1M 4AA, for the extract from the *The Listener*, 24 October 1946.

Bloodaxe Books for the extract from *Pencil Letter* by Irina Ratushinskaya.

Burns & Oates, Wellwood, North Farm Road, Tunbridge Wells, Kent TN2 3DR, for the extracts from *Thoughts in Solitude* by Thomas Merton, 1975.

The Rev Jim Cotter, Cairns Publications, 47 Firth Park Avenue, Sheffield S5 6HF, for the extract from his book *Prayer at Night*, 4th edition, 1988.

The Church Missionary Society, Partnership House, 157 Waterloo Road, London SE1 8UU, for the extract from an article by Clare Amos in the magazine *Yes*, May–June 1988.

Cistercian Publications Ltd., WMU Station, Kalamazoo, Michigan 49008, USA, for the extract from *One Yet Two: Monastic Tradition East and West*, ed. M. Basil Pennington (Cistercian Studies Series No. 29).

Wm. Collins & Co. Ltd., 8 Grafton Street, London W1X 3LA, for the extract from Shakespeare's *Othello* in the *Complete Shakespeare*, 1968; for the extracts from *Lord of the Journey*, ed. Pooley & Seddon, 1986; and for the extracts from the Book of Common Prayer [no date given].

Darton, Longman & Todd Ltd., 89 Lillie Road, London SW6 1UD, for extracts from *Yes to God*, by Alan Ecclestone, 1975; *Iulia de Beausobre: A Russian Christian in the West*, by Constance Babbington Smith, 1983; *My Father Took Me to the Circus*, by Prue Wilson, 1984; *God of Surprises* by Gerard Hughes, 1985; *A Doorway to Silence* by Robert Llewelyn, 1986; and *Moment of Christ* by John Main, 1984.

J. M. Dent & Sons Ltd., Aldine House, Albemarle Street, London, for the poem *Love III* by George Herbert, ed. C. A. Patrides, Everyman, 1974.

Faber & Faber, 3 Queen Square, London WC1N 3AU, for the extracts from the *Four Quartets* by T. S. Eliot, 1970; *Murder in the Cathedral* by T. S. Eliot, 1965; and for the extract from the Puffin Book *James and the Giant Peach* by Roald Dahl, 1961.

The General Synod of the Church of England, Church House, Dean's Yard, London SW1P 3NZ, for extracts from the Psalms in *The Alternative Service Book*, 1980.

Grail Publications Ltd., 125 Waxwell Lane, Pinner, Middlesex, for the use of a story from *Living from Within* by Philippa Craig, 1979.

Hodder & Stoughton Ltd., Dunton Green, Sevenoaks, Kent TN13 2YA, for the extract from *A Celebration of Faith*, ed. Leslie Houlden, 1970; for the extracts from the poem "Faith" in *The Unutterable Beauty* by G. A. Studdert Kennedy, 1964; and from *The Hiding Place* by Corrie ten Boom, 1971.

McCrimmon Publishing Co. Ltd., 10–12, High Street, Great Wakering, Essex SS3 0EQ, for the extract from *Heaven in Ordinary* by Angela Ashwin, 1985.

A. R. Mowbray & Co. Ltd., St Thomas House, Becket Street, Oxford OX1 1SJ, for the extracts from *Praying Round the Clock* by Richard Harries, 1983; and *Letters of Direction* by the Abbé de Tourville, 1939 Dacre Press, A. & C. Black Ltd.

Oxford and Cambridge University Press, The Edinburgh Building, Shaftesbury Road, Cambridge CB2 2RU, for the verses from The New English Bible, 2nd ed., 1970.

The Oxford University Press, Walton Street, Oxford OX2 6DP, for the extract from *The Oxford Book of Prayers*, ed. George Appleton, 1985.

Penguin Books Ltd., 5563 King's Road, London SW19 0UH, for the extracts from *A Story Like the Wind*, by Laurens Van der Post, 1972; *Revelations of Divine Love* by Mother Julian of Norwich, trans. Clifton Wolters, 1966; and *The Cloud of Unknowing*, trans. Clifton Wolters, 1961.

SLG Press, Convent of the Incarnation, Fairacres, Oxford OX4 1TB, for the extracts from *Creative Suffering*, Pub. No. 88 by Iulia de Beausobre; *Silence in Prayer and Action* Pub. No 78, by Sr. Edmée; *Listening to God and Listening to Community*, by Mother Mary Clare, Pub. No. 69; and *God Under My Roof*, Pub. No. 87, by Esther de Waal.

The Society for Promoting Christian Knowledge, Holy Trinity Church, Marylebone Road, London NW1 4DU, for the extracts from *Marked for Life*, by Maria Boulding, 1985, and *The Edge of Glory* by David Adam, 1985, both Triangle Books; also *Beyond All Pain* by Dame Cicely Saunders, 1983.

Spes Sancta, Newbury, for an extract from a prayer-card, quoting Rev Mother Stuart.

The Tablet, 48 Great Peter Street, London SW1P 2HB, for the extract from an article by Fr. William Barry SJ, "Wrestling with God", 11 Aprl 1987.

71250 Taizé Community, France, for the extract from *Letter From Taizé*, May–June 1986.

The United Society for the Propagation of the Gospel, Partnership House, 157 Waterloo Road, London SE1 8UU, for the extracts from *Prayer is My Life* by Margaret Dewey (date not known).

Also available in Fount Paperbacks

Audacity to Believe
SHEILA CASSIDY

'A story of extraordinarily unpretentious courage in the horror of Chile after Allende's overthrow. It is easy to read, totally sincere and sometimes moving. Sheila Cassidy is totally disarming.'

Frank O'Reilly
The Furrow

Prayer for Pilgrims
SHEILA CASSIDY

'. . . a direct and practical book about prayer . . . has the freshness of someone who writes of what she has personally discovered . . . many people . . . will be grateful for this book and helped by it.'

Neville Ward
Church Times

The General Next to God
RICHARD COLLIER
'An absorbing, sympathetic record of the man (General Booth) and his family and the movement they created.'

Michael Foot
Evening Standard

Also available in Fount Paperbacks

BOOKS BY C. S. LEWIS

Christian Reflections

'This collection . . . deserves the warmest of Christian welcomes on
this happy reappearance . . . a devastating counter-attack on the
"new morality" and a magnificent restatement of the essence of the
Gospel and the faith.'

Church Times

The Four Loves

'He has never written better. Nearly every page scintillates with
observations which are illuminating, provocative and original.'

Church Times

Prayer: Letters to Malcolm

'A book full of wisdom, of bitter honesty and of deep charity. It
nowhere tells us "how to pray" but . . . stimulates afresh that hunger
and thirst for God without which we should never pray at all.'

J. B. Phillips

The Pilgrim's Regress

'A welcome reappearance in paperback. Bunyanesque in form, as
the title suggests, this reissue may well pick up a new generation of
readers . . .'

Methodist Recorder

Also available in Fount Paperbacks

I Believe
Trevor Huddleston

A simple, prayerful series of reflections on the phrases of the Creed. This is a beautiful testament of the strong, quiet inner faith of a man best known for his active role in the Church – and in the world.

The Heart of the Christian Faith
Donald Coggan

The author "... presents the essential core of Christianity in a marvellously simple and readable form, quite uncluttered by any excess of theological technicality."
The Yorkshire Post

Be Still and Know
Michael Ramsey

The former Archbishop of Canterbury looks at prayer in the New Testament, at what the early mystics could teach us about it, and at some practical aspects of Christian praying.

Pilgrim's Progress
John Bunyan

"A masterpiece which generation after generation of ordinary men and women have taken to their hearts."
Hugh Ross Williamson